AUBREY ON EDUCATION

The manuscript: Aubrey's additions to 'Relaxation and Bodily Exercise'

AUBREY
ON EDUCATION

A hitherto unpublished manuscript
by the author of *Brief Lives*

Edited by

J. E. Stephens

Department of Education
University of Hull

ROUTLEDGE & KEGAN PAUL
London and Boston

First published in Great Britain 1972
by Routledge & Kegan Paul Limited
Broadway House,
68–74 Carter Lane,
London EC4V 5EL
9 Park Street, Boston,
Mass. 02108, U.S.A.
Printed in Great Britain by
Butler & Tanner Limited
Frome and London

ISBN 0 7100 7218 X

Contents

v

CONTENTS

Preface

The *Idea of Education*, begun in 1669 at the Grange, the family home of Aubrey's close friend, Sir Robert Henley, took almost fifteen years to complete. Much of the manuscript is ill-arranged and repetitive, and despite the fact that the author returned to it at intervals to amend and to annotate parts of the text, it remains incomplete. There are several hundred insertions in the margins vertically and on the reverse side of the manuscript sheets. Many of the additions are no more than personal memoranda to the writer reminding him to seek out this or that paper or to ask advice on some point at issue: others record his second thoughts and the opinions of the virtuosi in whose company he mixed. That Aubrey was aware of the shortcomings of his work is evident from the draft of a letter, dated February 1694, which he prefixed to the introduction. The material needed an Aristarchus, he wrote, 'to consider in which place it would stand best.' Acting at his behest then, the text has been rearranged to give its disparate parts a unity which they would otherwise lack. Aubrey's original intention was to have thirty-three chapters:

ix

These have been re-grouped in three parts with the sections indicated in the chapter contents.

The longer interpolations in the main have been included where the author seems to have wished they should go; whilst the shorter jottings appear as terminal notes. Most of the classical allusions, aphorisms, couplets and *bons mots* have been included, either in the text, or in the notes. The exception is the comment of Horace, *lib.* III, *Ode* 4, which Aubrey uses to illustrate his view that training improves those who are already well-endowed intellectually: this has been used in the Introduction. Similarly, most of the longer extracts from other writers have been placed in the text where he intended. The more important of these have been identified in square brackets where Aubrey failed to acknowledge the source (for example, Chaucer's *Tale of Melibeus* and Milton's *Of Education*). A number are omitted; notably the printed pages, bound in the manuscript, from *Of Magistracy*, 1688, by Samuel Johnson, the rector of Corringham (1649–1703), and from *Resolutio triplex*, 1658, by Jonas Moore. Aubrey's short transcriptions from the preface to Christopher Wase's *Gratii Falisci Cynegeticon*, 1654, and of a problem from Sybrand Hansz's *Hundred Geometrical Questions*, 1644, have been left out, but three of the longer items have been added as appendices. These are selections from Milton's *Of Education*, 1644, which Aubrey knew in the 1673 reprint attached to the second edition of the Minor Poems, part of Thomas Newcombe's 1649 translation of Descartes's *A Discourse of Method*, and the whole of Samuel Foley's paper to the Royal Society.

Throughout, names have been systematized. Spelling and punctuation have been changed to accord with modern usage, except where this would destroy the flavour of Aubrey's style. Latinized names have been retained generally and may be identified more exactly in the biographical notes and in the index. Aubrey's several omissions are indicated by means of a dash: ellipses signify editorial omissions in the text.

Acknowledgment

I am indebted to the Bodleian Library, Oxford, for permission to publish John Aubrey's *Idea of Education* from MS. Aubrey 10, and for permission to reproduce the illustration of Aubrey's manuscript.

Introduction

The Restoration settlement, the political backcloth to Aubrey's essay, proceeded in two stages. The first, in 1660, saw the rehabilitation of the King and the ruling class. Appropriately, it was engineered by the Presbyterian Convention Parliament, for Presbyterians at this stage still formed a conservative and rigidly orthodox element in the Church. Between April and December they revised the previous order of society, replaced republicans and democrats with royalists, and substituted hereditary caste and ancient custom for a regime which had tended to favour talent more highly than birth. Concurrently, there was a marked change in attitudes towards schools and universities. In restoring the *status quo*, popular education became suspect. Society closed its ranks. Ascription, rather than attainment, became once more the key to social advancement. The apparent abundance of England's educational provisions was seen as one of the causes of the Civil War, for it was held that the supply of educated men had far outstripped the ability of the country to absorb them into positions of authority and responsibility in ordering the nation's affairs. The discontent thus released was seen to find expression in political action and in large measure was believed to have sustained the Cromwellian regime. What more natural than that in the post-Restoration conservative reaction, traditional control by traditional authorities should have been reasserted? The fears earlier expressed by Richard Mulcaster and Francis Bacon that education was undermining the values of established society were in the 1670s given a new form by Christopher Wase. His *Considerations Concerning the Free Schools, as settled in England* examined the view that discontent and subversion were intrinsic to the universities and schools. A number of Cromwell's major-generals had appeared to merit Wase's charge of 'men illiterate, beneath ingenious breeding'. It was difficult not to find a connection between the Puritan leadership and the grammar schools, for Cromwell himself had been educated at the free school attached to the Hospital of St John, Huntingdon, during the mastership of Dr Thomas Beard; John Bradshaw, president of the court which tried the King, was a product of the free schools at Stockport in Cheshire, Bunbury and Middleton in Lancashire; John Hampden went to Thame Grammar School, then under Richard Bourchier; and the Lamberts to schools at either Kirkby Malham, which a Lambert had endowed in 1598, or Skipton or Giggleswick, both equally near the family home at Calton. In fact, the Wase inquiry into the provision of schools produced no evidence to sustain the charge. The idea nevertheless persisted, largely because it accorded well with current antipathies towards social mobility and the advancement of the unworthy. It had a marked effect on the debates in both houses on the disputed Act of Uniformity, when the extension of the Act's terms to schoolmasters was cited 'as necessary for the proper education of the young, the neglect of which amongst the gentry and nobility was the root of the numerous mischiefs of the Long Parliament'.[1] At the same time, it coloured the writings of the educationists. It is only necessary to compare the works of John Tillotson, Isaac Barrow and Thomas Sprat, the historian of the Royal Society, with those of Samuel Hartlib, Hezekiah Woodward or John Durie, to appreciate the extent of the changes that had taken place since the Restoration.

Of more immediate and trenchant consequences to education was the second stage of the Restoration settlement; that associated with the return of the Anglican Church, militant now in the cause of Parliament rather than the King. Ironically, the Presbyterians who, in the 1660 Parliament, reaffirmed the dominance of the traditional ruling class, failed completely to realize that this would in turn be followed by an ecclesiastical settlement in which they would have no part, and as a consequence of which they would themselves become in the space of a decade fragmented and sectarian. For whatever else was restored in 1660, it was not the earlier Arminian connection between King and Church. The divine unity no longer existed: in post-Restoration England the idea of royal power under God as the basis of the traditional scheme of society played little part. At the same time that authority was restored, the Presbyterian insistence on the importance of the individual's part in religious experience and the necessity for direct and personal knowledge of the Bible disappeared. Since it was apparent that universal literacy for this end was unobtainable, the movement towards primary education for all petered out.

Moreover, irrespective of religious and political considerations, the later seventeenth century was marked by a declining birthrate, particularly amongst the upper classes; by the closing of the free market in land which had followed the release to purchase of crown and church estates; and by an increase in patrimony in the church, in the guilds, in civic government, and in the law factors which, in a hierarchic society set on retrenchment and consolidation, were stabilizing in their effects.[2] The obligations of power thus firmly based were evident enough to the writers of the period: the upper classes must furnish society with men of talent. They must be persuaded to resume their responsibilities.

Of the proposals for institutions like Aubrey's, those of three contemporaries and associates are worth noting. Similar to Aubrey's own scheme was that of Sir Francis Kynaston (1587–1642), poet, scholar and barrister, who about 1635, as a leading figure in a talented literary circle at Court, founded a *Museum Minervae*, where a wide range of subjects could be studied, from the accomplishments of athletics and the chase to skills of public administration. To what extent the academy prospered is uncertain for it met opposition in the universities, and its author died hard on its inception. John Evelyn's proposals, first promulgated in a letter to Robert Boyle in September 1659, also had features in common with Aubrey's. Evelyn saw a need for a college near London. They were 'not to hope for a mathematical college, much less a Soloman's House, hardly a friend in this sad Catalysis', but he was prepared to sink some of his own capital in the venture, a gesture the impecunious Aubrey could not match. He planned a monastic regime, built round the discipline of prayers, study, conversation and fasting. He conceived of a small estate within twenty-five miles of the capital, containing a large pavilion, with study rooms, a refectory, pallet sheds, gardens, laboratories, arboretum and conservatory, costing some £1,600 at most. There he and his wife were to lodge in separate apartments (for they were to be 'decently assunder'). In return he was to furnish the buildings at a cost to himself of £500 for seven years,when it would become public stock. It was to be a modest establishment in comparison with that Abraham Cowley described in his *Propositions for the Advancement of Experimental Philosophy* of

3

1661. This was to have an annual revenue of £4,000 and support twenty philosophers or professors, sixteen young scholars, a chaplain, bailiff, manciple, two gardeners, a surgeon, two lungs (or chemical assistants), a librarian who was to be a druggist and keeper of scientific instruments, and a retinue of menial domestics. Its constitution accorded equal status to all the professors, and the obligation, on a rota basis, of foreign travel for four of them, 'to give constant account of all things that belong to the learning, and especially the natural and experimental philosophy of those parts.' Of the remaining sixteen, two, by turns, were to teach in the public school. All were to engage in experiment and keep a close register of their findings in those fields of study which Bacon had laid down in the *Organon*; namely, mathematics, mechanics, medicine, anatomy, chemistry, the history of animals, plants, minerals, elements, agriculture, architecture, military science, navigation, gardening, the mysteries of all trades, the manufacture of all merchandise, natural magic and divination. One-third of the profits from their discoveries were to go to individuals, two-thirds to the Society. Its buildings were to resemble those at Chartreux. There were to be three courtyards or quadrangles, one attached to the living accommodation, the second to the domestic offices, kitchens, buttery, brew and bake houses, stables and dairy, the third to the teaching block—public lecture hall and assembly rooms, library, display gallery, dispensary, anatomy chamber, mathematical instrument room and public school house.

Aubrey's intention was to set up a number of schools—'seven such colleges in England would be enough'—with up to sixty scholars in each, near London at Kensington, at Merton in Wiltshire, at Cranborne in Dorset, at Oxford, in North Wales, in Glamorgan and in Lancashire. It seemed possible that the Earls of Leicester and Pembroke and the Marquis of Worcester might have endowed such establishments, for like designs had already found sponsors. Evelyn's proposals of 1659 to form an academic community within twenty-five miles of London had attracted attention in Ireland, where a thousand acres were promised for its support, and in Northamptonshire Lord Newport planned to convert to a similar use Fotheringhay College, the teaching society founded by Edward, Duke of York. Samuel Hartlib's passion for the Utopian Macaria, a convention of the great, the wealthy, the religious and the philosophical in a common centre for promoting literary effort and Christian unity, was not a spent force when Aubrey's *Idea* was taking shape, for the Viscountess Ranelagh, sister of the physicist Boyle and the Earl of Cork, and her associates Robert Wood and Hannibal Potter, worked towards its accomplishment. More important, Cowley's *Propositions for the Advancement of Experimental Philosophy* had hastened the establishing of the Royal Society. There were other obstacles than the lack of financial support, however.

From the time of the publication in 1531 of Thomas Elyot's *The Gouvenour* and the anonymous *Institution of a Gentleman* in 1555, it is clear that, in theory and practice, institutions intended for the education of the nobility were more progressive than the established grammar schools. James Cleland's *Institution of a Young Nobleman*, 1607, Henry Peacham's *Compleat Gentleman*, 1622, Durie's *Education of Nobles and Gentlemen*, c. 1646, and Jean Gailhard's *Compleat Gentleman*, 1678, in their various ways described programmes of training and courses of study of a most advanced kind.[3] To a large degree, the explanation of this state of affairs is to be found in the extent of the Church's supervision, for the Church's role in school education in the seventeenth century was extensive and influential—increasingly so after the Restoration. It had a position, derived from medieval canon law and statutes, which made it the most effective single organ of control over sources of ideas and enlightenment and over youth aspiring to some position in society by virtue of talent. From the same sources it derived its licensing authority and it kept a tight hold on entrants to the professions. It had a direct responsibility in those establishments which were administered by the deans and chapters in the cathedral cities, and elsewhere its officials superintended education in their capacities as visitors of schools, appointers and nominators to vacant masterships. Under the Canons of 1604 its curates could teach school in those areas where others had no prior right. Moreover, the hierarchical structure provided for a measure of control over education at all levels. The bishops in their dual capacities as servants of church and government were able to influence decisions in both parliament and convocation, while their surrogates, aided by visitation machinery and the ecclesiastical courts, executed their decisions. At a more humble level, clerics served as private tutors. The nobility in Aubrey's view were in the clergy's pocket. As individuals, churchmen played a prominent part in the early activities of the Royal Society and in societies for the reformation of manners; they provided parochial libraries, taught in the university colleges, travelled and experimented. Like all large institutions, the Church contained men with widely differing views on education as on everything else, and it is possible to trace after 1660 extremes of conservative and radical opinion in the pronouncements of churchmen, as it is during the Interregnum. What is apparent after the Restoration, however, is the existence of a body of vaguely educational and social theory concerned with the school curricula, the duties of parents and children, family life, discipline, the poor, charity, etc., held by a majority of churchmen, which in today's terms would be described as right of centre—to such an extent had the social and political climate changed. Collectively then, in its institutional capacity, the Church seemed a threat to educational advance. Aubrey's own scheme, he felt, was jeopardized by the 'dark squadrons'; more particularly by John Fell, Bishop of Oxford.

If the various proposals are separated from the extracts from Milton, Descartes, John Pell, Israel Tonge and others which Aubrey incorporates in his text, they fall into three parts. The first and shortest deals with the purposes of education and current practice, and is intensely critical of the heavy classical content of the curriculum and the tyrannical quality of much of its teaching. 'It may perhaps seem paradoxical to aver that no gentleman's son in England is so ill-bred (or can have so good a breeding) as the King's mathematical boys at Christchurch Hospital in London, but it is certainly so.' Yet 'arithmetic and geometry are the keys that open unto us all mathematical and philosophical knowledge, and by consequence all other knowledge: sc. by teaching us to reason aright and carefully, and not to conclude hastily and make a false step.' What was in fact taught, Aubrey concluded, had the contrary effect. 'As for grammar learning, the commonest way of teaching it is so long, tedious and preposterous that it breaks the spirits of the fine, tender, ingenious youths and makes them perfectly to hate learning; and they are not to be blamed for it. Most of their rules which they commonly learn are as difficult to be understood as a logic or a metaphysic lecture, and the authors they read as hard to be understood as any they read when they come to be men. Besides, there is beating and dispiriting of children from which many tender and ingenious do never recover again. In this respect Aubrey's views are close to those of the foremost Puritan educators, particularly Comenius. His dictum that education should be carried out not with severity or any kind of coercion, but easily and, so to speak, by its own momentum, is characteristic of their contribution to educational method in the middle of the seventeenth century, which envisaged a teaching programme where the natural desire to learn would be encouraged: it meant a reappraisal of traditional school practices and

6

was based on a new approach to Latin and a reduction of the number of hours children spent at school. The teacher might also be expected to show gentleness and appreciation in the schoolroom, and to furnish its buildings adequately and pleasantly. The *Analytical Didactic*, which appeared seven years after his visit to England, abounds in fruitful ideas that only gradually pervaded educational thinking. In it Comenius urged that despotism and terror should be banished, that learning should be motivated through pleasure, and that schoolmasters should teach only what the scholar could grasp, and this by carefully graduated instruction, freely given. He wanted to cultivate the average mind by teaching in the mother tongue, and to bring culture to the masses.

Similar principles in one form or another can be seen in the theory and practice of most of the Puritan educationists of the Commonwealth period. Although Hartlib's attempt to have Comenius undertake the reform of the educational system was thwarted by the Civil War, he succeeded in keeping Comenian ideas alive. In 1654 he published *The True and Ready Way to Learn the Latin Tongue* and dedicated it to Francis Rous, Speaker of the House of Commons, in the hope that it would be well received by the Committee for the Advancement of Learning. Durie pressed for the setting up of Christian communities, authoritarian and co-operative, whose common purse would provide a school for every fifty boys. Learning was to be unforced, and individual, in the sense that it was held to be the master's duty to discover the aptitude and temperament of each child. Similar views occur in John Hall's *Humble Motion and Petition to the Parliament of England*, in the pamphlets of Samuel Harmar and in the anonymous *Chaos*. In the Utopian *Nova Solyma, the Ideal City: or Jerusalem Regained* no one with natural endowments of a higher order was allowed to remain unnoticed and neglected because of the obscurity of his birth. 'Nor are the less gifted despised on that account and reckoned unworthy of much educational care; indeed we use special efforts in their case that they may be able to raise to the full height of their capacity and in due course fitly perform their duties to the state.'

If, through his familiarity with educational texts and his acquaintance with those who had advocated the reform of schools and universities, Aubrey's work displays a similar humanity, with their programme of social reform he had little sympathy. His upbringing as a member of a county family, well-connected with government by virtue of minor state and ecclesiastical preferments, did nothing to convince him of the efficacy of the Puritan case. Consequently, the socio-religious theories of the 1650s receive no consideration in the *Idea*. It is interesting that Hartlib, the ubiquitous influence behind all the educational ventures of the 1650s, is mentioned only in the context of his connection with Milton and Lubinus, and that Adam Martindale, who was associated with classical presbyteries in Lancashire and Yorkshire, should figure as a successful teacher of mathematics and Latin.

In the second section Aubrey deals with school government and organization. A provost, a well-travelled, unmarried layman, would preside over the school—'a fair house with a little park, high-walled of about a mile about'—and its inmates. There were to be three informators, 'not one of these to be an Englishman, but chosen from Switzerland and Scotland', who would teach grammar, rhetoric, logic, civil law and ethics; an oppidan to teach drawing, some ten or twelve Swiss, Dutch or Scottish boys of about fifteen years of age, bound by a six-year contract, to assist with mathematics and to instruct in Latin by the direct method. The entourage would consist of a governess, 'a discreet, well-bred gentlewoman that is unmarried and has no daughters', a butler 'to be a barber to shave their heads to keep 'em from lice', a French cook, scullions proficient in Latin and a lusty Swiss porter with a 'decent livery and a long sword' and a facility in modern languages. The school routine is explicit; even to the details of food, sleep and exercises. If boys erred they were to be punished by the removal of privileges or with finger-stocks, rather than by severe beating, for 'a school should indeed be the house of play and pleasure and not of fear and bondage.' Aubrey's own early experiences remained with him and he attributed the headaches from which he suffered throughout his life to the chastisement he had received from his schoolmasters. 'I very well remember', he writes, 'that excessive whipping when I was a little child did make a convulsive pain in my tender brain which doubtless did do me a great deal of hurt. 'Tis a very ill thing to cross children; it makes them ill-natured. Wherefore let them not be crossed in things indifferent. 'Tis a pity that this indulgence is not used by schoolmasters.' The school library, the matrix of the community, was to be outside the control of both the provost and the informators, and to prevent the kind of embezzlement which occurred at Blandford, his own school, Aubrey would have duplicate lists of books deposited with the lord lieutenant of the county or in some great house nearby.

The third part of the *Idea* contains details of the courses of study.

Aubrey was not inclined to accept Sir William Petty's view that 'twenty men are enough to do all the Latin business of England', for Latin was the universal tongue and no man was well-bred who was ignorant of it. Nevertheless, arithmetic, mathematical prudence, geometry and algebra were essential. John Newton, the minister of Ross in Herefordshire, who kept a mathematical school there, had demonstrated the delights of mathematics well taught. Aubrey would have his teachers interpose bodily exercises suitable to their strength and age, and, he decreed, 'let them change studies; for example, from grammar to mathematics, from writing to graphics.' In addition, he outlined a course of study in ethics, logic, rhetoric, civil law, politics and economics, and he suggested paradigm examples of solutions to problems in these fields. How many years students would spend at the school was clearly a matter about which Aubrey reached no firm conclusion. He recognized that some boys quickly reached an age when single-minded dedication to study was impossible: 'the only time of learning is from nine to sixteen; afterwards Cupid begins to tyrannize; jealousies, marriage and worldly cares intertwine with studies.' The French academies served as an example of the mistake of keeping youths at their books too long—'great fellows, at an age more proper for matrimony, when their minds do chiefly run on propagating their race. Nature will be nature still at 18+. So that at this age, and with these circumstances, their information is like writing on greasy parchment: it will not stick and leave an imprint. Or, like painting anew on an old picture, the new colours will not be imbibed.' Nor would he have them come to school too early: between nine and twelve seemed best, provided their early training had followed the precepts of his *Idea*, which advocated a gentle initiation into the world of language, books and self-discipline. He would have children educated 'at home under their domestic nurses, who might be so instructed that by teaching the young children they might learn themselves'. At four they could be expected to know pleasant songs to 'exercise their tender young memories with delight' and 'give them a habit of speaking plain and clear: to vowel their words, as the songster terms it, and make them have a graceful and Italian-like pronunciation which we English do generally much want.' He would dispense with the hornbook and introduce reading and writing *via* Comenius's *Ianua Linguarum* and Israel Tonge's method. On number teaching he was an eclectic, borrowing freely from contemporary writers and from the opinions of Edward Davenant, Sir Christopher Wren, Edmund Halley, William

Oughtred and Thomas Ax, whose early mathematical training he carefully recorded.

On the question of the nature and incidence of intellectual capacity, the view, widely held by Aubrey's contemporaries, Richard Allestree, Isaac Barrow and Edward Veal, *inter al.*, in the 1660s and 1670s, was that all men were equally educable.[4] Tillotson, some years before his elevation to Canterbury, had contended that 'in many things, and these the greatest things,' differences were of little account. His sermons on equity in men's dealings with one another examine in detail the concepts supporting ideas of equality and human potential. The following extract from 'Wherein lies that exact righteousness which is required between man and man' is characteristic of this position:[5]

As to abilities of mind, which we usually call parts, there is originally a great equality, especially if that received opinion be true, that souls are equal; and, as the French philosopher, Des Cartes, hath ingeniously observed, there is this noble sign of the equality of men's understandings: '*nulla res*', saith he, '*aequabilius inter homines distributa est quam bona mens*'. Men will acknowledge others to be richer and stronger than themselves; few will acknowledge others to be wiser, or have better parts than themselves. Now because all men generally think thus, it is to be presumed that all are not deceived, but that there is some real equality, which is the ground of conceit. A difference, indeed, must be granted, but which ariseth usually from one of these two causes—either an unequal exercise of our parts, or an unequal temper of body.

That there was selection, and that some progressed further than others, was fortuitous. Heredity—that is, inherited social advantage rather than physical and psychological endowment—was important only in that it gave the gentleman access to those experiences which would enable him to develop his potential to the full. But since his function was to rule this was only common justice. Leaders of society, magistrates, landlords on their estates, gentlemen of leisure, had the duties of their stations: they were obliged to differentiate between the true and the false in politics and religion; they must therefore be educated. In so far as these functions were not expected of those who, by chance, or by some great design, had inherited inferior social positions, there was little point in putting them to school. With these sentiments Aubrey was in broad agreement. Yet he recognized with delight that

exceptional talent could be discovered in the most unlikely places—
a boy in his tenth year who did strange things in arithmetic; a barber's
apprentice who had a prodigious gift for music; a carpenter with inventive mechanical genius—and was anxious that it should be cultivated. Hence:[6]

> Doctrina sed vim promovet insitam,
> Retique cultus pectora roborant
> Utcumque defecere mores
> Indecorant bene nata culpae.   Horace, *lib.* III, *Ode* 4.

These, in short, are the proposals contained in the *Idea of Education
of Young Gentlemen.* They arise out of a preoccupation of the author
with the neglect of schools, particularly by the nobility. If the system
of private tutoring had any virtue, Aubrey was not aware of it. 'Young
heirs, bred at home, are so flattered by servants and dependents of the
family that they think themselves to be the best men in the nation, and
they are not to be blamed for it, for they know nothing to the contrary. . . . Besides . . . their minds are advocated with continual suggestions of trivial divertisements as coursing, hawking . . . which are
alien in this way of education that I propose.' Unlike Thomas Sprat,
historian and fellow member of the Royal Society, who shared with
Aubrey a vision of applying new techniques to usher in a future of
unlimited wealth, he was convinced that change should begin in the
schools. That the well-to-do should be educated in a more public
setting than hitherto, he had no doubt. On the other hand, his proposed schools, scattered throughout the country, were to be in no
sense as socially comprehensive as the grammar schools and most of
the great schools had traditionally been. Gentlemen, in Aubrey's
estimation, were the fittest persons to breed gentlemen, and youths
of quality ought to be brought up among their equals. 'A cobbler's
son may have a good wit and may perchance be a good man, but he
would not be proper for a friend to a person of honour. It is of ill-
consequence for a youth to be sent to a great school in his own
country. . . . Schoolfellows know one another's foibles, as they say,
and some come to be their servants who were their playfellows at
school.' His school community, then, was to be highly selective, and
closed, in the sense that no remove to a university, other than Leyden,
was envisaged 'except it be to some peculiar college of law or physic
where they mean to be practitioners'. Towards Oxford and Cambridge
his attitude was ambivalent: he had hopes of the mastership of Glouces-

ter Hall (later Worcester College) and clearly admired the handful of brilliant alumni, Isaac Newton, Thomas Hobbes, Christopher Wren, Edmund Halley, John Ray, Robert Hooke, William Petty, John Wilkins and John Wallis. He was, however, aware that the universities were surpassed as centres of teaching and research by the nonconformist academies and the Royal Society. These may not have enjoyed the same endowments and opportunities, but they displayed a disproportionate share of intellectual vigour. Aubrey retained a belief, also, in the value of proficiency in Latin as one of the ends of education and such reforming zeal as he was capable of went into attacking methods of teaching and into achieving a more sensible balance between the classics on one side and science and mathematics on the other.

In practical terms, his scheme came to nothing. He found no wealthy sponsors and he did not enjoy the satisfaction accorded to other educational writers of the time—the Wottons, Henry and William, Obadiah Walker, Stephen Penton, Bathsua Makin, Thomas Tryon, Thomas Baker and Robert Ainsworth—of seeing his work in print.[7] Only recently has interest in Aubrey revived. He has emerged as more than an amiable, and at times scandalous, gossip as the extent of his contribution to Wood's *Athenae Oxonienses* and his antiquarian studies of Wiltshire and Surrey have been recognized.[8] His essay on education is a fascinating repository of nostrums and sound practice, partly his own, partly those of the men of letters and science who shaped post-Restoration society.

Part I

[To John Evelyn]

Sir,

In case I should happen to die before I call for this *Idea* I desire that you leave it with Dr. Hooke at Gresham College to be put into my chest marked *Idea*, which is full of books for this design.

Sir, I pray God help you and yours,
                Your very faithful and
                    humble servant,
                        John Aubrey
May 10,
    1692
[Postscript]
Here are some things put down in two places. I know it very well; but because it is easier to strike out than to interline I let it stand to consider at second reading in which place would be most proper.

[To Anthony Henley]

                                London, Febr. 27, 1693/4
Sir,
    I hope this child of mine will be presented to you in a lucky hour. I am much joy'd to hear that excellent character you give the Earl of Leicester. He may be a means to promote this design. The Earl of Pembroke has read it all over and excerped some things; he approved

of it, but is not active. I wish I may live to transcribe a fair copy (next March I shall be 68), from which others may be transcribed. I have some hope that the Marquis of Worcester, to whom my brother is well known, may propagate this design in Wales. I am not over-confident of my Lord Weymouth. It would be but, as it were, saying Fins [*finis*] to the E[arl] of P[embroke], Lord W[orcester] and Lord Ashley, to have it established at Cranborne: but God's will be done. If the nobless have a mind to have their children in the clergy's pockets, much good may it do 'em.

Some nations are down twice: they should be but once. But I desire an Aristarchus (that is your kind self) to consider in which place it would stand best. If I chance to die before you return me the book, be pleased to leave it with Dr. Hooke at Gresham College, where is a great chest on which is writ *Idea*, in the library which is full of books relating to it.

But I foresee that if I die they will lie coffered up, and no body have that generosity as to set afoot this noble design.

I pray God bless you and prosper you. I am, with all my heart
  Sir,
    Your faithful friend and humble servant.
[Postscript]
In case I may serve you in anything, be pleased to direct me. To be left with Dr. Gale, schoolmaster of Paul's School.

I

Proem

Plato says that the education of children is the foundation of government: it will follow then that the education of the nobles must be the pillars and ornament of it. 'Tis true there is an ample provision made in both our universities for the education of divines, but no care has been taken of the right breeding up of gentlemen of quality, than which there is not anything of greater moment in a nation; for it is the root and source of their good administration of justice. It may perhaps seem paradoxical to aver that no nobleman's son in England is so ill-bred (or can have so good a breeding) as the King's mathematical boys at Christchurch Hospital in London, but it is certainly so. About 167–,[1] King Charles II erected that Mathematical School for forty boys to be made fit for navigation, but their teacher is on the King's order to teach no other. But we want such a nursery, or way of instruction, for the children of the gentry.

As for grammar learning, the commonest way of teaching it is so long, tedious and preposterous that it breaks the spirits of the fine, tender, ingenious youths and makes them perfectly to hate learning; and they are not to be blamed for it. Most of their rules which they commonly learn are as difficult to be understood as a logic or a metaphysic lecture, and the authors they read as hard to be understood as any they read when they come to be men. Besides, there is a tyrannical beating and dispiriting of children from which many tender and ingenious do never recover again. I have known some that forty years old and upwards when anything troubled them, they dream't they were under the tyranny of their schoolmaster. So strong an impression does the horror of the discipline leave.

This tyranny at Blandford School was so great that yet, upon any trouble Captain Baynard dreams he is there at *hic, haec, hoc* with fear and trembling, which was about thirty years hence. The like for twenty years by dreams, frequently happened to myself.

It was a most ridiculous and imprudent way of breeding up youth in King James's time or before, and at Bristol much used as yet, *viz.* to damp poor lads' spirits, and so daunting them with whipping, cuffing and brow-beating that oftimes a spirit thus broken never recovers itself again. This way made not only a strangeness between parents and children, but made the child absolutely to hate the parent, as a rogue the bedel. What a sad thing it is to see youths or girls come before strangers, hanging down their heads, sneaking and void of spirits; whereas nature intended at this age their eyes should dance with joy. One thus spoiled, 'tis well if he recovers his understanding faculties but to speak in public without being confounded with fear. Being scared, and having other ideas than which he should have at that present presenting themselves to his imagination, he will never be able, but either do it with angry ill-grace or leave off in the middle of it.

Now rather a child of mine should undergo such slavery, he should never learn the Latin tongue, but be content with that of his mother, and be mathematically informed. John Newton, D.D., minister at Ross in Herefordshire, kept a mathematical school there for youths who did profit exceedingly under him. He protested to me that, after they were a little entered, they took so great a delight in their studies that they would learn as fast as one could teach them. But he was utterly against the learning of the Latin tongue at this school: he would not have the studies mixed. Methinks he was too straight-laced and magisterial in that point, for since it is so that Latin is the universal language, and that one cannot be said to be a well-bred man that is ignorant of it, I should think it fit that their studies be inter-mixed and changed with delight. But their Latin should be learned after an easier manner. Mr. Martindale, a nonconformist schoolmaster in Cheshire, teaches both and with very good success, and is the only person that I hear of that does so. They take a great delight in it and on play days make it their pastime.

Arithmetic and geometry are the keys that open unto us all mathematical and philosophical knowledge, and by consequence, all other knowledge: *sc.* by teaching us to reason aright and carefully, and not to conclude hastily and make a false step. These two sciences ought to be instilled into boys and they will joyfully imbibe such demonstrative delightful and useful learning. And being learnt so young, it sticks by them as long as they live, and becomes habitual. Otherwise, when these two sciences are learnt by men of good years, as commonly it falls out, it turns the edge of their wits, and they give it off. Or, if not, they make no great matter of it. For example, Mr. Thomas Hobbes, who was forty years old or better when he began to study Euclid's *Elements*. 'Tis as though a man of thirty or forty should learn to play on the lute when the joints of his fingers are knit. There may be something analogous to this in the brain and understanding. Sir Jonas More told me that he had a Fellow of a house in Cambridge that was one of the best humanists and orators in that university to be his scholar for mathematics, thirty years old and more. He protested he could not make him understand or learn division, and so he gave it off as incapable.

Without a doubt, it was of great advantage to the learned Mr. W. Oughtred's natural parts that his father taught him common arithmetic perfectly while he was a schoolboy. The like advantage might be reported of the reverend and learned Edward Davenant, D.D., whose father, a merchant of London, taught him arithmetic when he was a schoolboy. The like may be said of Sir Christopher Wren, Mr. Edmond Halley and Mr. Thomas Ax, whose father taught him the table of multiplication at seven years old.

As for private education, though great persons are able to maintain able instructors, the inconveniences are so many and so obvious that 'tis needless to recount them. Young heirs, bred at home, are so flattered by the servants and dependents of the family that they think themselves to be the best men in the nation, and they are not to be blamed for it, for they know nothing to the contrary. So when they make their entry into the world amongst their equals and superiors they give offence and become ridiculous, till time, and affronts, and perchance some beatings, have more civilised them. Besides, being bred at home, their minds are advocated with continual suggestions of trivial divertisements as coursing, hawking, setting and conversation with their sisters and relations, domestic differences—all which are alien in this way of education that I propose, and where they will be weaned from their nursery.

The French academies seem to me not able to perform the generous education promised thence, and so much cried up. 'Tis like the shearing of hogs: they make a great cry and little wool. The most considerable thing learned there is to fit to be a man, a French chevalier, to manage the great horse; that is in plain English, to be a complete trooper. 'Tis true, there are masters for mathematics, for logic, for the lute and ghitarre, and all these are learnt and jumbled together when they are great fellows at an age more proper for matrimony, when their minds do chiefly run on propagating their race. Nature will be nature still at eighteen +. So that at this age, and with these circumstances, their information is like writing on greasy parchment: it will not stick and leave an imprint. Or, like painting anew on an old picture, the new colours will not be imbibed. However, the boys at St. Omer have an *ingenistitium* at grammar that indeed they have very well. The like is at La Flêche and the rest of the schools of that Society [the Jesuits]. The reason is plain. Because they are not made acquainted with the sweets and illicibrations of the sciences (e.g. arithmetic and geometry), nor are they well introduced into the knowledge of the passions, but pick up scraps out of the old poets.

'Twas a great disadvantage to me in my childhood to be bred up in a kind of park, far from neighbours, and no child to converse withall, so that I did not speak till late. I was eight years old before I knew what theft was, for I had a fine top which was stolen from me. My father had one to teach me in the house, and I was pent up in a room by myself, melancholy. At twelve years old I was put to public school at Blandford under Mr. W. Sutton, B.D.;[2] I was like a bird that was got out of his cage amongst the free citizens of the air. It was the first time I knew the world and the wickedness of boys. The boys mocked me and abused me that were stronger than myself so I was fain to make friendship of a strong boy to protect me. I am sensible of the inconvenience of my former private education to this very day, besides it impaired my health. Sir Christopher Wren said also the same of himself; wherefore he has sent his son to a great school, Eton, not much caring what Latin he learned, but to learn how to shift and live in the world.

Now for the remedying of a private or pedantic education there must be taken a quite contrary way of institution for breeding up youths of that rank. Gentlemen are the fittest persons to breed gentlemen, and youths of this quality ought to be bred up among their equals. Here at school are laid the fundamentals of friendships and acquaintance which last till death. A cobbler's son may have a good wit and may perchance be a good man, but he would not be proper for a friend to a person of honour. It is of ill-consequence for a youth to be sent to a great school in his own country, which contracts an acquaintance never to be shaken off, and this will be chargeable as well as perpetually troublesome. Most men do not desire to have a glass before their hearts that all people might know their minds and affections. What is the disposition of a boy is the same when he is a man, only he covers it with a vizor of cunning and dissembling. Schoolfellows know one another's foibles, as they say, and some come to be their servants who were their playfellows at school.

Part II

The Institution

I would have a fair house with a little park, high-walled, of about a mile about.

A provost, or controller, who should be a gentleman and well-educated, and that has travelled in France, Italy and Germany: a layman and unmarried, and an irrevocable order made that neither the provost nor any of the informators should marry, for if they should, their daughters would debauch the young gentlemen, not to say worse, to become their wives. Then all the art in the world cannot undo it. I know some great heirs that have been undone in this way (e.g. Sir Francis Rolle's only son).

I would have three informators in grammar, *sc.* one to every class for the convenience of examining them and correcting their exercises; and not one of these to be an Englishman, but chosen from Switzerland and Scotland: to be men of presence and *bôn mine* and behaviour, not little contemptible Rattons [rats] such as gentlemen commonly take into their houses and are ridiculous to the foot boys.[1] Besides their ability in teaching, I would have them to be of sweet and even tempers, to study and find out the tempers of the boys, and to have the gift of teaching. For want of this good sweet temper many ingenious and tender spirited youths are spoiled. For example, that learned knight, Sir Henry Spelman, was like to have been had he not left his master. 'Tis not qualification enough for the informator to be a learned man, but it must be principally considered that he be a good natured man, not rough and austere and dogged, to kill and fascinate children with his angry eyes. Van Helmont says that the spirit of a malicious person does really hurt and make sick the party maliced, and children are more susceptible of this spiritual venom or malignity than more adult persons. A boy will never learn well of a teacher that has an antipathy to him.

A mathematical teacher. A rhetorician that may be a Scot. One of the informators of grammar to be a censor of their oratory and translations. A logician, who should also read them the rudiments of civil law and ethics.

I would have the salary of the informators to be an hundred pounds per annum apiece: and their chambers free and, if it might be afforded, their commons, which would be a handsome livelihood.

Ten or twelve Swiss or Dutch or Scottish boys (French boys will be naughty) of about fifteen years old that speak Latin well, to play with and instruct the young gentlemen, and to exercise their speaking of Latin. I would have them bound for five or six years. They will also be useful assistants in the mathematics and may make useful persons in their generations, and first to travel with their young gentlemen beyond the sea. They may succeed the informators of the school in vacancies. They may prove, having travelled once or twice, very good governors (as they call 'em) to young gentlemen that travel. They may become good officers and stewards. After four or five years I would have English servitors (boys) to be bred up in this college.

The cook, a Frenchman or Swiss; as also the scullions, to speak Latin. The butler, a Swiss, to be a barber to shave their heads to keep 'em from lice. A governess, a discreet, well-bred gentlewoman, that is unmarried and has no daughters, to oversee the nurses and woman servants and to take care of the young gentlemen.

The porter should not be an old fellow in a gown, like an old fool to forget men's names and errands, nor a scabby old, sneaking servant with a tattered gown like a scarecrow. But I would have a lusty young Swiss with a decent livery and a long sword: one that can speak Latin well and readily, as many of them can, besides the French and German tongues. This porter may be a tailor and r'accomode their clothes. Such a one had his excellency, my Lord Denzil Holles, ambassador at Paris.[2] Several such are to be found.

I would not have the number of young gentlemen more than fifty or three score at the most. I would have at least half a dozen such schools established in England and Wales. One at Canbury House at Islington,[3] where are lodgings enough, the air not bad and area enough, with a wall fifteen feet high, according to the rhyme:

> Sir John Spenser for stealing a calf,
> Built a wall a mile and a half.

The great city of London would bear it to have another at Kensington, or in Surrey. Kensington is too near the roads, e.g. Hyde Park. There should be one in the north of England about Lancashire. The Earl of Shaftesbury's house at Merton in Wiltshire would be a very pretty place, delicate airs, but too little for a school for fifty or sixty gentlemen. But the Earl of Salisbury's house at Cranborne in Dorsetshire, where the family has not lived for about seventy years, would be the finest house in England. Gloucester Hall in Oxford would be a good place for one of the schools, but it would be envied by the other colleges.[4] There should be one in north Wales; another in Glamorganshire which lies very convenient for Somerset, Devon and Cornwall, a very cheap county, and healthy. The house of Richard Lewis, Esq., not these many years inhabited, where there are a great many little rooms and good air would be as good a place as could be found.

The Lord Chancellor Bacon in his book, *The Advancement of Learning* says, 'All these things are to be held possible, and performable, which may be accomplished by some persons, though not by everyone, and which may be done by the united labours of many, though not by anyone apart; and which may be furnished by the public care and charge, though not by the ability and industry of particular persons.' There is no doubt to be made but that if two or three public spirited persons did undertake to establish this useful design it would bring them more profit than £6 or £8 per cent. I would wish it begun at Canbury House; if not, Sir Thomas Fisher's house [also at Islington] would do well enough. Next, I am for Glamorganshire for sweetness of air and cheapness of provisions and 'tis but a short way from Somersetshire and Devon. This institution must be established by the gentlemen of the county, for if it should be set up by schoolmasters, cheating and oppression would certainly follow. Methinks Mr. Richard Waller and his brother-in-law, Mr. Pitfield, both very ingenious and rich, were fit persons to begin this near London. In Glamorganshire also are many men of great estates, if God would put such a work into their heads.

The place should be at once both school and university, not needing a remove to any other house of scholarship except it be to some peculiar college of law or physic where they mean to be practitioners.[5]

Visitors and Electors

For the schools near London, the Lord Keeper, the Lord Bishop of London, the Lord Mayor, the two Chief Justices, the Judge of the Admiralty and the President of the Royal Society or Vice President, with a delegacy of Fellows.

For the schools in the countries [i.e. counties], the Lord Lieutenants, the Bishop of the Diocese, the Deputy Lieutenants, Justices of the Peace and Quorum.

For the election of the informators would be most proper the President of the Council of the Royal Society and the teacher of the King's mathematical boys at Christchurch Hospital—I mean for mathematics.

Could I have my wish, I would have a provost or controller for the school near London to see discipline observed, who should be a well-bred and prudent person, and unmarried, who ought to have a noble salary allowed him for careful overlooking them. I do not know anyone who is better qualified for such a one in all respects as my honoured friend Mr. Peyton Chester, who is an admirable algebraist and very well understands civil and canon law.

The visitors to choose the governess, who is not to have a daughter with her. The servant boys, or apprentices, to be preferred after such a time, when they are superannuated; *sc.* to travel with the gentlemen beyond the sea, or to succeed as an informator. But let them be chosen by the ballot of the young gentlemen.

I find by experience that feoffees and trustees and the like are careless and negligent to meet upon public business unless there is something of eating and drinking in the case, which is an allurement to meet. Wherefore, I would have here yearly a feast for the visitors to meet and make inspection into the management of the informators and scholars, provostess or governess, to hear freely complaints. Surely they will be willing to meet. Surely, they will be willing to meet at such a joyful feast, for I know not what meeting on earth can administer more joy.

But I foresee this design's like to be opposed by the clergies of both parties, but it will find some champions and supporters; for example, George, Duke of Buckingham; Aubrey, Earl of Oxford; Thomas, Earl of Pembroke; Francis, Lord Guildford, Lord Keeper; Henry [Compton], the Lord Bishop of London; the Earl of Dorset; the Earl of Craven; the Marquis of Halifax; James, Earl of Abingdon; John, Lord Vaughan; Seth, Bishop of Sarum; Sir William Petty; Sir James Shaen; Thomas Povey, Esq.; and many other members of the Royal Society.

3

Government

The stage of adolescence, seventeen, eighteen, nineteen and twenty, is an ungovernable age: lust does then pullulate, and they do grow *in venerem*.[1] They have the strength of men, with boys' heads. But ingenious young gentlemen thus educated (but the emphasis ought to be put on the word 'ingenious') will be more ravished with the pleasures of knowledge, which to intellectual complexions of all pleasures is the greatest, than those brutish ones of the sense.

Dr. Kettle, the vigilant President of Trinity College, Oxford, said that the great arcanum of government (out of Seneca) was to keep down juvenile impetuosity; but then you must begin with them at nine, else you will not keep down their obstinacy.

In the universities in Scotland the rule is whilst boys are boys, to govern them as boys and keep them strictly to their studies. When they are grown young fellows, 'tis time for 'em to leave the school and launch out into the world. Sir Thomas Overbury, who wrote a pretty little treatise *Of Education*, 8° stitcht, says that the French leave off books at sixteen, which he thinks to be two years too soon, but he complains that the English hang on them too long. I have said before that the pure fundamental learning is obtained between the years of nine and sixteen or seventeen inclusive. But to go further, as to the laws or divinity (which last is not here concerned) it must be mastered by the age of twenty-five years, for afterwards the management of his estates will take up most of his time, besides visits and returns of visits. *Qui habet terras, habet guerras.* Besides it is the time of wife and children, law suits, justice of the peace business, so that now his estate has rather him, than he his estate. 'Tis now evident if he keeps up the knowledge he treasured up in his youth, and adds his own observations.

I would have the economy of the bees to be observed in this school and idleness banished, for such as have not the ethereal fire will never do themselves good here, but they will do others hurt. One cannot be idle alone; wherefore, let the drones be put hence to their parents.

As I would not have the undertakers of this design to be losers, so I would have all imaginable care taken and provision made that the gain should be the thing chiefly aimed at. Now whereas the common way of schools is for gain's sake to keep their scholars under the tuition as long as they can, as physicians and surgeons do their patients, I would have this illustrious institution so prudently ordered by the visitors that those oppressive tricks and cheats should find no room to enter. In order to which I would have every informator to have an honourable salary paid him quarterly, so that, whether there are more or fewer scholars their gains are the same; and being all laymen they are to be interest only in this their business.

Neither controller nor informator to be a married man, and I would have this to be most religiously and inviolably kept. Nor any young maidservant to belong to this society, for nature will be nature still, and there is no fencing against it. When youths do not see young women, they do not think of them. 'Tis needless to speak of the inconvenience of married schoolmasters, as also heads of houses. Their wives too often make matches with young heirs to their daughters or relations, and this is not uncommon. Not to make a long enumeration of such mischievous contrivances, the only son of Sir Francis Rolle and grandson to the Lord Chief Justice [Henry] Rolle, had his education under a seeming-godly nonconformist at Newington who married him to his neice that lived with him. My honoured and ingenious friend, William Neile, Esq., R.S.S., son and heir of Sir Paul Neile, Knight, was like to have been married to his schoolmaster Dr. Triplett's daughter had it not been timely discovered.

No informator to stand by when another reads, which is a good rule observed in the academies at Paris. They say one master is enough at one time. It binds the child's fantasy and awes him. Suppose the grammatic or civil-law informator has in mind to learn the mathematics, let him ask questions and be instructed at some other time.

At fifteen, let 'em by turns, go along with the cook and manciple into the market to see the buying of the provisions: to be stewards, as in the halls and some colleges in Oxford, for which let 'em have some privileges as they have there. They will see the world and know how the market goes without hearsay, and learn to know good flesh and fish from bad and stale; for example by the breaking of the bone to see the freshness of the blood, if young.

A discreet matron, well-bred, to look after the children and take care of them and their linen. An able and experienced nurse from London for the smallpox and measels, to attend them, who might assist the governess.

Caution money to be delivered at the entrance of any gentleman.

The porter to walk about the lodgings every night to see that their candles are put out, for example, as at the Jesuit colleges.

The master and scholars to be bareheaded when they speak to one another, as at the Society of Jesus.

There should be a provision made and care taken for the apprentices —outlandish youths, when they are super-annuated.

Consider if it be not the best and cheapest way to pay honourable salaries to the informators; for example, £100 per annum as at Christchurch Hospital to the mathematical master, than for the informators to receive money of every one of the scholars in particular: for avoiding the inconvenience of keeping the scholars too long under their own hands for their own gain, as at our grammar schools.

As to their habit, it should be decent and fashionable according to their quality, but not luxurious for the avoiding of pride, envy and emulation—the first things put into children's heads in the nursery, which ill-weeds, if possible, ought to be eradicated. But as for lords' sons, they are not within this predicament: they should all wear Indian gowns and taftan caps, especially in the winter. Not to be dressed à la mode till dinner time.

It would not only be cleanly, and for the saving of time that is taken up in combing their heads, and for the preventing of lice, which are apt to swarm in children's heads, but I believe conducible also to their health and wit, to have their heads shaven.

Let the children sleep out their full sleep; otherwise follow rheumes and catarrhes, oscitations and therefore dulness, till the perspiration is performed. Besides, to make them rise before that is over will stint their growth. This rule was practised by the Right Honourable [Elizabeth], Countess of Berkshire in ordering of her children, who are all healthy, beautiful and ingenious. Some friends of mine impute their unhealthiness to their too early rising at Westminster School.[2]

Orders or Statutes

No scholar to be disturbed at his lecture by any stranger visitant.

No scholar to go without the walls with any visitant but a parent.

Not to rise too early (especially in winter) because it checks their perspiration and so dulls them; and it stunts their growth.

No lecture to be above half an hour (by an hour glass) for their eager spirits should not be put upon the fret and be tired. When they learn it should be with a quick and keen appetite.

The intermixed recreations to be but for half an hour.

To observe justice strictly, *Sc.*, *quod tibi fieri non vis allis ne feceris*.

To debellate pride, arrogance, mocking, envying, affronting.

Their habit to be decent and fashionable but not luxurious, which will cause envy among them.

The scholars not to be beaten about the head.

Every informator and apprentice to be bound in a bond-penal not to set up a school within forty miles of the place where they teach.

No oppidans to be admitted to learn here for they will spoil their well speaking of Latin.

The orders of the school to be like the laws of the Medes and Persians never to be broken.

The statutes of some colleges do prohibit *musica instrumenta* because noise disturbs the fancy and frights away notions. For example, Sir Miles Fleetwood, Recorder of London, riding by the horn maker's at Fleetbridge, the boy blew a horn as he was intent upon some business concerning Queen Elizabeth. He used some passionate expression, that the boy had blown the Queen's business out of his head. But upon times of relaxation, I would have those young gentlemen that have musical inclination to enjoy their fancy.

Penances and Punishments

For the honour of the school, and for that there should be nothing here of terror or gehenna to fright youths from the love of learning, I would have no such thing as the turning up of bare buttocks for pedants to exercise their cruel lusts. That worthy and gentle schoolmaster, Mr. Gardiner of Blandford, was wont to say that the calling of a schoolmaster was next to that of a divine, but for that beadle's office of whipping.

> As pedants out of the boys breeches,
> Do claw and curry their own itches.

In Spain (or Portugal) the schoolboys for faults have shackles put upon their legs, such as their slaves wear, and are sent with them home through the streets.

The fathers of the Society of Jesus do whip the calves of their scholars' legs.

I would have finger stocks, such as were in the old time in gentlemen's halls; for example, at the Earl of Carrington's in Warwickshire.

To stand in the middle of the school.

To be prisoners in their chambers.

To be kept at their books, when their fellows are at play.

Not to rusticate and ride abroad when others do will be a great penance.

The apprentice boys to be whipped by the porter.

4

Relaxation and Bodily Exercise

For exercise, the tops and gig, but especially the shuttlecock, which is an introduction to tennis, quickens the eye and prepares to fencing. Besides it is not too violent, yet robust enough; and children ought to be exercised to digest their phlegm and [dispel] their moisture, consequently amending the temperature of their brains. Let anyone observe when he has played at shuttlecock or tennis (I mean moderately) whether, when he comes to study, he does not find his understanding and apprehension clearer than usual. It disperses the fog which in England is frequent. Monsieur Balzac makes this topic sound high:

> and he, Madam, who hath discovered all the truths of heaven
> and was ignorant of nothing that could be known without
> revelation, made so particular an esteem of it in his fourth book
> of Ethics, that he was not afraid to say that sport and
> divertisement were no less necessary to life than rest and
> nourishment. *The Roman.*

Wherefore, let every Thursday (especially in the afternoon) be a time of relaxation from their other tasks. Let 'em walk in the fields, or ride, but still to be kept strictly to speak good Latin: sometimes (rarely), in their short journeys to visit persons of quality, but never to lie out except upon extraordinary reason.

Here should be kept half a dozen or more little horses for the young gentlemen to ride out by turns. I would have the gentleman of the horse to be a well-bred Swiss who speaks good Latin as most of them do and had seen the wars, to teach the young gentlemen to sit a horse gracefully and discourse to them of the world and of wars, and to

34

delight them: to mind them of N. Machiavelli's observation in his *Prince*, which is what Philopoemen did long ago, namely, when he did ride abroad he would consider the ground, so, and so; if an enemy were there how should he order his strength.[1]

Young men do much want airing, especially those of sulphurious complexion: they are apt to kindle a fever without it. Good air is a *pabulum animae*: when they do air themselves, either riding or walking, let them be informed in the botanics and husbandry (good or bad) as also antiquities if they lie in their way; and therefore let an old antiquary or botanist travel with a young man to inform him. Some of them will catch at these things. Let 'em carry in their coat pockets Mr. John Ray's *Synopsis of English Plants*[2] or Mr. Paschal's *Botanic Tables* from Mr. Ray's book done in the Real Character[3] in three sheets. The Duke of Orleans and several great princes and persons have made it their delight and recreation. Methinks it is a kind of irreligion to be ignorant of the names and virtues of those plants that grow about our dwellings, which we daily see and with which we are daily nourished. Those who are easy enough may read Virgil's *Georgics* and Servius's *Notes* and let 'em peruse Columella and Varro *de hiis* that they may be the better acquainted with them hereafter if they have a mind to it. Mr. John Evelyn affirms that none have writ better. He says that out of them are to be extracted all good rules of husbandry, and wishes that a good collection or a broad general were made out of them. I wish they would read them, as likewise Plautus, for the overcoming of a hard Latin word is like Lord Bacon says, '—'tis like wearing lead in ones shoes, that afterwards makes one go more light'. Dr. Ridgeley tells me there is a book written in High Dutch by Colerus in folio which is the best upon agriculture. 'Tis a pity it is not translated. This will give 'em the sense that they need not be altogether governed or hoodwink't by the stewards or bailiffs when they are men. Baptista Porta's *Villa* would be very fit for their reading: 'tis an admirable book.[4] 'Tis proper for a gentleman to know soils. As they follow their botanics, let 'em make notes of the earth and minerals, in rocks and on the surface as also the witherings in corn or grass which is by the breathing of a mine. To travel at several times over all England and Wales, observing as aforesaid, as also engines and the like, and let them enter them *in adversariis*.[5] To see the sea and harbours and rocks or cliffs will be a strange sight to them, and will exalt the fancies to see—*qua brachia longo margine terrarum porrexerat Amphitrite*. (Ovid, *Met.*, *lib.* I.)

'Tis good to show the children all manner of rare sights, for example at Bartholomew's Fair or the like, to give them an impression of an elephant, tiger, crocodile, *etc.* They see colour with other eyes and hear sounds with other ears: all their senses are more nice and subtle. Their tender brains receive the fragrant odour of plants with great pleasure; their skins are thin and tender, and the pain of whipping is beyond all other: it brings convulsions and makes 'em fools. Youth should be indulged as to all lawful pleasures.

Perpetually to read men and to observe their manners and humours and (as an appendant hereto), not to neglect observations of physiognomy. There is also a judgement to be made of one's disposition. See *Philosophical Transactions,* about 1679, *de hoc.*[6]

Let 'em bear in mind the admonition of Father Drexilius, *sc. semper excerpe,* to which purpose, let everyone have about a little paper book. This will be a nest-egg. They will in a short time be pleased with the increase of their stories and 'twill bring them to a habit to continue it as long as they live. At night to give an account of their observations that day, always observing the laws of common justice, civility and decorum.

For such an illustrious school, there ought to be a tennis court as well as a ball court. For the youngest youths, till twelve or thirteen, shuttlecocks and tops and scourge are moderate and wholesome exercise. Paper kites are ingenious and 'twill please them to fly them in the autumn. The little chariot with three wheels at Bunhill Fields, invented by a cobbler, which is driven by a crank is very good exercise for the arms and body; 'twill teach them to steer a coach or a ship and be a hint to other inventions. In the court or garden I would have a noble basin, as that in the quadrangle at Christ Church, Oxford, whose diameter is over forty feet, deep about four feet and a half, to learn the art of swimming, and to wash themselves in warm weather.

As for those children whose geniuses carry them on strongly to practical music, I would have them practise first two plain parts, *viz.* treble and bass, and next three plain parts and no more; to tune and settle their ears that they will presently discover if their companion plays not a true note. Methinks that more than three parts makes rather a confusion than harmony. I would introduce them into the gamut by the keys of the organ or virginal, and by rote, not so hard as the Paternoster. It is to a prodigie what a proficiency a child that is musically or paintingly inclined will make when they are taken in their due time. Our Vicar's daughter, Abigail Slop, played in consort

W. Lawes, his base's three parts when she was not fully six years of age: she wanted one month of it, this to my knowledge. When they come to some mastership, I would have them make commonplace of harmonical figures and chords and to excogitate the reason why such and such affect the mind with joy, or sadness. Without a competent skill in practical music, the theoretical part can not be so well learned or understood as it should be. There are left undiscovered to us yet, no doubt, very useful and curious things that may be elicited from harmonical proportions, fit for the learned to make search of.

'Tis a just complaint of music that it is too great a thief of time; but that that is not consistent with prudence as some too severe and saturnine complexions affirm may be repelled by several illustrious examples. Henry VIII, Rex Angliae, was a good musician: he composed a song in eight parts which is mentioned in histories, and in Mr. Butler's *Of Music*. The Landgrave of Hesse was a master in this art and a composer. Ussher, Lord Primate of Ireland; the learned Dr. Sanderson, Bishop of Lincoln; Mr. John Milton; Bulstrode Whitlock; Sir Francis North, Baron of Guildford, Lord Keeper of the Great Seal was an admirable musician, but I remember that he told me that he learnt it so young he could hardly remember it: it was so habitual to him.

Mr. Christian Smyth, organ-master—a German—says that an organ of three stops is enough for a chamber organ, and to sing to. They should also have a harpsicall or spinett, or both.

I would have as little fiddling as may be, and that only by those who have a great and strong inclination to music, for it is a great thief of time and engages men in base company of pimps, fiddlers and barbers. And when they have taken all the pains they can, whose daily practice it is, a barber's boy, or a foot-boy fiddler shall equal them, if not outdo them. What a sad and unseemly thing it is to see one of thirty or forty years learning on the lute, violin or organ, and though he might have been as good a proficient had he learned in due time as anyone, that time being past both for habitual and for the pliableness of his muscles, he thrashes to his own displeasure and great vexation whilst he might have spent his time much better. *Musica mentis medicina*, or when they are wearied with study, but then this must be the habitual way; for example, as the Honourable Francis North and Colonel Danvers.

Peruse Sir William Petty's advice, that those who have mechanical heads (which will quickly be discerned), let them on play days and vacancies, practise drawing, painting, turning, grinding of glasses for telescopes and watchmaking, to which I will add the tin-man's trade, which is easily learned and requires not above three or four tools, the use whereof is that those who have mechanical heads will be able to make models of their own ideas and inventions themselves. The Lord Marquis of Worcester had a very mechanical head, but I doubt he wanted good information in the mechanics. His grandfather understood the smith's trade and shod his own riding horses. His Highness, the Prince Rupert, was an excellent gun-smith; as also is Sir Gabriel Lowe of Newent in Gloucestershire.

Let them not be ignorant in cookery which the French understand well, for in travel or in the army it is of good use.

Before they leave this education, I would have those that have ingenious souls go through a course of chemistry that they may not be altogether strangers to that useful art, and will draw them on to improve their knowledge in their travels in Germany.[7]

Every night after supper I would have them play at cards, the youngest to begin with One and Thirty. This will fix their numbering and addition thoroughly. Then I would have them introduced to some other easy game; then to Cribidge, Gleeke and Picquet, and so upwards to Pocket Primero and Primoriste, which last two, though never out of fashion, are the most masculine games and exercise the judgement more.[8] This conduces to number and also to have a foresight in the management of their affairs. To Draughts (Mr. Latimer), but more especially the game of Chess, in order to which, for the A,B,C of it, they are to learn Fox and Geese which Ludovicus Vives in his *Dialogues* teaches; as also to play at Ruffe. This will seem, I fear, to be strange advice. I would be as unwilling as anyone to have my son make a trade of gaming, but this knowledge is of more consequence than most men are aware of. Gamesters are the best managers of their business of all others. It opens their heads and prevents cheating if they have a gaming ascendent, and makes it habitual in them to have a foresight and forecast in all their actions of great importance.

Robert Stephens of the Middle Temple, Sergeant at Law, was wont to say that playing at cards did open children's understanding: the same said Sir Francis Ritter of playing at chess, that it made them to have a foresight in the world. And Sergeant Stephens observed that good gamesters, did manage their law-suits with more prudence than other men. Great statesmen are generally gamesters, e.g. Cardinal Mazarin, an excellent gamester; so M. Colbert, Thomas Hussey, Esq., the great purchaser; Sir John Maynard, Sergeant at Law, and so is

Sergeant Stephens himself. His father would have the cards brought into the parlour every night after supper for the children to play, till such an hour, nine or ten.

I would have them learn to dance of a French dancing master, the sooner the better, as in all things. It makes them have a good gait, and qualifies them for the conversation of ladies and keeps them from the drunken order. One would think that this qualification were very foreign as to a soldier, but it is not so, for it makes a commander to tread a good step and to march with a bôn grace before his company. To learn dancing when they come to the university or the Inns of Court is of dangerous consequence, for to these schools do resort the handsome young wenches with whom they do contract an acquaintance, and sometimes marriage. Country dances are a good diversion in the winter season. I had rather have them dance with country lasses, than silk petticoats. I would have them on gaudy days to *indulgere geniis* with a modicum of pure, good wine, French or Rhenish, for thin wine does clear the brain, and refreshes the spirits and is a good medicine against the worms. It is observed that those children who are too severely prohibited to drink wine do generally prove drunkards.

They may have a bank for wine, of the money that is won at play every night. I remember Dr. Fell, Dean of Christ Church, Oxford, if he found a young gentleman in a tavern, he would chide him very mildly, but if he caught him in an alehouse, he would be very severe to him.

5

Chambers

In every chamber I would have some good sentence in letters which they will remember as long as they live. This was much the fashion in the old time, and in the old windows of colleges before the civil wars, as 'arcanum cela quod dubitas ne feceris'.

The chambers in the Jesuit colleges have all the like furniture, so that when you see one, you see all. They are hung with green bayes which refreshes the eyes, with a fillet of gilt leather in the seams. But I would have Sir Francis Bacon's fashion followed, when Solicitor General, whose chambers at Gray's Inn were hung with grass-green say [serge-like cloth] and I think a gold fillet, but in the middle was some pretty emblem with a motto finely touch't with a pencil upon white sattin, in an oval of about sixteen inches the long diameter, encompassed with two palm-branches knit in a knot below, embroidered, and then sowed upon the say, which looked very fine. The windows should have clear glass panels which do clear and comfort the spirits. *E contra*, the old fashion'd dark, monkish windows depress their spirits and make them heavy and melancholy: but it served for the intention of monkish mortification.

I would have the maps of the four parts of the world in every chamber; an olive chest of drawers and Dr. Wilkin's cuts of the Real Character [prints, presumably, from engraved blocks or plates].

Two that have an antipathy to one another, not to be in the same chamber; 'twill put 'em upon the fret, and they may mischief or kill one the other.

The guard screens for the fire should be planispheres.

Hall

In the Lord Chancellor Bacon's hall at Gorhambury at the upper end of the table is the picture of an oak with acorns and some men below eating of them, to put us in mind of our ancestors. And in another picture is Ceres teaching men to sow corn, and cultivate land, and underneath thus:

> . . . bene erat iam glande reperta,
> Duraque magnificas quercus habebat opes.
> Prima Ceres homine ad meliora alimenta vocato
> Mutavit glandes utiliore cibo. Ovid, *Fasti, lib.*, iv.

I would have fine florid landscapes, some whereof should have prospects of Rome, Tivoli or Caerphilly Castle to heighten and enliven their fancies.

The Portico

The wall of the portico at Gorhambury is embellished with ingenious pictures, as the sea, finely furled, and a ship entering into the Hercules Pillars: the motto *alter erit tum Typhis*.

Their Diet

For their breakfast, water and gruel, no milk, for Dr. Loss, M.D., a learned man, did affirm that whitebread and milk did certainly breed worms in children. Milk makes their bellies ache, and it curbs their inventions. For example, how dull are the dairy people that live upon whey and curds. In the winter time they may drink chocolate for their breakfasts. Tea will bring the diabetes, much used; and coffee makes their stomach heavy.

Moderate commons of mutton, beef or pork, when in season, not roasted beef, for it will make them sleepy; pottages, pease, artichokes, tarts and custards or cakes. Their table beer to be thoroughly boiled. I could wish they would use at meals pure spring water in which they would not be tempted to exceed. Fruits of the best according to season of the year to please their palates and to cool and refresh their brisk young blood. Let them not eat much.

Let there be drawn a bill of fare for every day in the week with relation to the seasons of the year and the months, as to fruits. But still remember to keep up their beef stomach which the wholesome country air with frequent exercises and rustications would do. By beef, I do not mean fresh beef, but finely cured and salted. Black-fowl does not breed good blood. Rabbits once a week (Sunday nights) are enough; 'tis too high a nourish for youths. I would not have them used to chicken and capons except in sickness when their stomachs are weak: if cordials are used too frequently, when they need them they do not so much good.

Whereas at most great boarding schools they do buy black muttons, stale flesh and fish for cheapness, which breeds diseases in children (though their parents pay sufficiently for good wholesome diet) I would have an especial care taken for the buying of wholesome viands. In order to which, besides the knowledge of the *achaterer* I would have two of the young gentlemen go as stewards with the cook or manciple into the market as is the manner in all the halls and some of the colleges in Oxford: this will acquaint them with marketing and make them know, not only the prices, but good meat from bad.

Advise what way is best for them to be dieted; whether to pay quarterly, as at boarding schools, or to battle as at the universities. I suppose it is best to battle only for tarts, fruit and wine, and half a pint not to be exceeded. In the colleges the commoners are much opposed in their battling. The exorbitant dear rates for boarding at Westminster School and other schools about London is a great grievance, namely thirty pounds per annum; twenty-five pounds per annum at the least, and yet the children have not their bellies full, nor perhaps what they feed on, fresh and wholesome food, but stale meat condited to take away the scent. This dwarfs them, stints their growth and fills them with disgust. The children of the first or lowest class should be under the instruction of the governess as to their diet. In this school will be avoided the tricks of entrance, giving pieces of plate, fairings, newyear's gifts, oppressing to parents.

The Chapel or Oratory

It were fit that such a school as this, where are so many young persons of quality, should have a neat-built chapel. I would imitate my Lord Bacon's here as in former rooms; *sc.* I would have at the east end the picture of Gratitude taken from the *Aurea* of Lairesse, namely a modest and beautiful virgin pouring frankincense into an aurum with live coals. Underneath is writ: '*Gratitudo*' and beneath that I would have this of Cicero: '*Religio est justitia nostra adversus Deum*'. I would also have here a small organ of these three stops, *silicet*, the diapason, the flute and the fifteenth; they follow one another, and are stops enough for a chamber organ, and to sing to. Among so many youths there will be found some good voices. On Sundays and on holydays I would have one of the young gentlemen or servitors to sing a hymn or anthem to a soft stop.

Hymns, the principal and ancient service of God are much neglected, and in its stead are used petitions and thanksgiving for ourselves. Mr. Edmund Waller, poet, said that poetry was never so properly used as in hymns; and when it was turned to other uses it was abused.

I would have musical notes set to Metrum. IX, lib. iii Boetii *de Consolatione Philosophiae, sc. O qui perpetua mundum a ratione gubernas,* and sung to the organ: as likewise Sir William Petty's excellent paraphrase on the —— psalm in Latin, printed in a single [sheet], and several other good anthems as *Non nobis Domine, non nobis, sed nomine tuo de gloriam,* or *Te Deum laudamus* by St. Ambrose which is thus translated into English in the *Hours* of the Roman Catholics:

> *Te Deum laudamus* (*translated*)
> Thy glorious name we magnify
> From age to age eternally.
> This day sweet Lord we now are in,
> Preserve us from committing sin.
> Have mercy on us Lord; efface
> Our sins with thy especial Grace.
> Thy mercy on us Lord be seen,
> As in thyself our hopes have been.
> Lord, I have fixed my hope in thee,
> Then let it not confounded be.

Two prayers composed by Sir Francis Bacon, Baron Verulam, Viscount St. Albans. The first prayer, called by his Lordship

The Student's Prayer

To God the Father, God the Word, God the Spirit, we pour
forth our most humble and hearty supplications, that He,
remembering the calamities of mankind, and the pilgrimage of
this our life, in which we wear out days few and evil,
would please to open to us new refreshments out of the
fountains of His goodness, for the alleviating of our miseries.
This also we humbly and earnestly beg that human things may
not prejudice such as are divine, neither that from unlocking the
gates of the sense, and the kind of greater natural light,
anything of incredulity, or intellectual night may arise in our
minds, towards Divine mysteries. But rather that, by our mind,
thoroughly purged and cleansed from fancy and vanities
and yet subject and perfectly given up to the Divine oracles,
there may be given unto Faith, the things that are Faith's. Amen.

The second prayer of his Lordship, called

The Writer's Prayer

Thou, O father who gavest the visible light on the first born
of Thy creatures, and didst put into man the intellectual
light, as the top and consummation of Thy workmanship, be
pleased to protect and govern this work, which, coming from
Thy goodness, returneth to Thy glory. Thou, after Thou had
received the words which Thy hands had made, beheldest
that everything was very good; and Thou didst rest with
complacency in them. But man, reflecting on the works which
he had made, saw that all was vanity and vexation of the
spirit, and could by no means acquiesce in them. Therefore, if
we labour in Thy works with the sweat of our brows Thou
wilt make us partakers of Thy vision and Thy Sabbeth. We
humbly beg that this mind be steadfastly in use, and that Thou,
by our hands, and also by the hands of others, on whom Thou
shalt bestow the same spirit, wilt please to convey a largeness
of new alms to Thy family of mankind. These things we
commend to Thy everlasting love, by our Jesus, God with
us. Amen.

44

The daily examin of conscience

The first point is to give God thanks for the benefits received. The second, to demand Grace, to acknowledge hate and leave our sins. The third to demand an account of our soul of the sins committed the day past, running over all the hours of the day since our uprising. And first of all in thoughts and in words, works and omniscience. The fourth to demand pardon of the sins we have committed. The fifth, to purpose to amend with God's Grace and help.

An Advertisement for the Morning

First, when thou awakest, pray to God, that He would so illuminate thee with the light of His Holy Spirit, that thou be not enticed to commit sin, and consequently seduced to death.

Prayer to be said at your awakening

O Holy Trinity, one God, etc., defend me this day from the deceits and temptations of the Devil; keep me from all mortal sin, and preserve me from sudden and unprepared death. Raise up, O God, my body from drowsy sleep, and my soul from sin, to praise and glorify Thy Holy Name, to whom belongs all benediction and honour and wisdom and thanksgiving, now and for ever. Amen.

At your uprising

Bless O Lord, govern me, keep me, and confirm me in all good works, this day and ever; and after this short and miserable pilgrimage, bring me to everlasting happiness.

Prayer for the night

Here examine your conscience and confess truly your sins by thought, word or deed.

Of these, O Lord, my sins, I repent me and am heartily sorry. I praise and magnify Thy name for the great, innumerable benefits particularly for preserving me this day. I beseech Thee for Thy protection this night to come, from fearful dreams and terrifying visions.

Prayers

At their first desertion of sleep I would have them use some short, pious ejaculation. Dr. Donne's *Devotions*, or Dr. Browne's, will furnish them. I would have them get into the habit of ejaculatory praying. When they are ready and come into their respective schools, I would have 'em begin with prayer, but the form to be short, and in Latin: a short thanksgiving and a blessing on their studies. The long, morning church service puts a damp upon their spirits. One keen hour's study as soon as they are up, is worth three hours at another time. The Jesuits have a saying, *qui studet, orat*. They wisely consider how much time the other orders lose in their chapels: but here their solemn going to prayers in the chapel or oratory should be a little before dinner or supper. Now the way of students in the universities is that they rise at or before six, then they go to prayers in a cold chapel; then they walk in the fields an hour; then they go to breakfast and then commit themselves to their studies, which must needs be with cloudiness and oscitation. What a preposterous way this is. On Sundays they may read Prudentius; 'tis a good pious book, now and then a false quantity.

The first rule that children should be taught should be 'do as you would be done to.' 'Tis very short and easy to be understood: if you do not so, you are unjust, a sinner, wicked. This little rule is the basis of right reason and justice, and consequently all other virtues. For want of observing this rule we see how strangely and brutishly we live among one another.

There ought to be made for these youths a rational catechism. Mr. Tho. White of Essex made a pretty one which begins thus: 'Child, how old are you?' Resp. 'Eight years old.' 'Child, where were you twenty years ago?' Resp. 'I was not born then, and consequently, nowhere', and so on, with an ingenious climax that leads the child to an understanding of a deity and creation. Sir William Petty has made a very pretty, short catechism for his children without any hard words of the schools. Ask my Lady Petty for it. Let them make observations of God's judgements upon oppressors. For example, the gentlemen in Northamptonshire that depopulated [i.e. as a result of their enclosures]: none of them have thriven. The like in Buckinghamshire. Plutarch in his tractate, *de Numine*, says that perjury and sacrilege go not unpunished in this life. I would have them learn the Real Character and the Real Religion.

The adage says *Oportet discentem credere*, but this should no longer be in force than till they come to eighteen years of age: afterwards let them use their own reason. We are taught our religion by our nurses and pedants, but when we are become men, Fortunatus Licetus says, every one makes a religion to himself.

Part III

6

The Cursus

Before a young gentleman came to this school, I would have a pre-
paratory education at home under their domestic nurses and govern-
esses to facilitate the work here, who might be so instructed that by
teaching the young children they might learn themselves. And first of
all when children are about four years old, I would have their nurses
teach them to sing pleasant short songs. This may seem frivolous but it
is not to be despised for that it will exercise their tender young memories
with delight and will give them an habit of speaking plain and clear; to
vowel their words, as the songster terms it, and make them have a
graceful and Italian-like pronunciation which we English do generally
much want. Some mothers and nurses have told me that children that
have musical souls will learn a tune before they can speak.[1]

I do not approve of the method used in the teaching children their
letters by the horn-book, or primer, in the black, purple and gothic
character which they may never perhaps have any use of in their reading hereafter, except they be common lawyers. The Latin character is
not only the most useful but the most simple and consequently the most
used and therefore the fittest for the first impression in the young child's
memory. The old black letters are derived from these with some
alteration, but the capital letters are so disguised and embellished with
knots and towsures as they may happen to puzzle a critic in the learned
language: 'tis like Ovid's expression,—*et pars minima est ipsa puella sui*
[*Rem. Amoris*, 344]. Wherefore it ought to be the Latin character
which they should first learn, but I would have it taught in that manner
as my friend Mr John Davenant was taught, which was this. His
father's man loved him and took him into his chamber when he had

raisins and comfits for him to allure and encourage him, and every day taught him one letter in some printed book, but every day repeating the letter or letters formerly learned. He would show him, for example, the letter A: 'this is called A; find me such another', which, running along the line he would quickly, and then was glad. By this method the child was taught to read in a short time. The boy being at that time towards five years old, the reverend Doctor, his father, and mother considered it was time to send their son to school. They put a primer in his hand to learn to read when he came to the school and began to show him the A B C, and he could read perfectly and they knew it not, which surprised them. When a child is after this manner perfect in his letters, he should be furnished with a spelling book (which was first invented by——).

St. Paul gives a precept to parents not to be bitter to their children, less they discourage them.[2] The Italian translation of Diodati renders it more emphatical: 'so less ye dispirit them'. The same is to be applied to the schoolmaster. Dr. Busby has made a number of good scholars but I have heard several of his scholars affirm that he has marred by his severity more than he has made. When children's spirits are thus cruelly broken they do never recover again: they are not fit to live in the active world, but for a monastic or collegiate life. Sir Matthew Hale, Lord Chief Justice, shows that the grief of children is exceedingly great and that many times they do never recover their dejection of spirits as long as they live—*experto crede Johanni*. Their pleasures are greater and their pains are greater. I very well remember that excessive whipping when I was a little child did make a convulsive pain in my tender brain, which doubtless did do me a great deal of hurt. 'Tis a very ill thing to cross children; it makes them ill-natured. Wherefore let them not be crossed in things indifferent. 'Tis a pity that this indulgence is not more used by schoolmasters. Mr. —— the schoolmaster of Gloucester, doth study the humour of his boys.

The illustrious Dorothy, Countess of Sunderland, whose wit and beauty is recorded to posterity in Mr. Waller's poems, gave her son by her second husband —— Smith, the best education that she could, and best advice as to morality and virtue, but would use no violence to the breaking of his spirit, but said that she left that to God's grace, and disclosed she left his natural morals to God's guidance.

I would have their nurses begin to teach them number at five or six years old and when they do begin to read, not put 'em to read the Bible as the common way is, but I would have 'em instead of that to read J. Comenius's *Ianua Linguarum* in English, with little pictures which will leave a strong impression and serve for local memory; and to read it over two or three times and by that time the impression will be well fixed. And then when they read it again in Latin or Greek they will learn it much the better and sooner. It will be like *stratum super stratum*, and they will never come to any study or science that will be strange to them. Also, while they do learn to read, or before they read the *Ianua*, I would like them to read Mr. George Sandys' translation of the psalms, or other English poetry, as his Ovid's *Metamorphoses*: the verses do trammel them, and tune their ears; and then after a little while they will stop as true and read truly and not endure a false word. This I do know by the experience of friends' children of mine.

Now as for the age when youths should be sent to this school, I would not have them come before nine, or admitted after twelve years old. If after twelve, they grow too hard and strong and wilful: the ill-habit they bring with them is with great difficulty unlearned, and they will do a great deal of hurt to the other youths. Mr. J. Ward said by experience that the only time of learning is from nine to sixteen; afterwards Cupid begins to tyrannise; jealousies, marriage and worldly cares intertwine with studies and confound them. Before nine Mr. Ward finds to be too soon. He has now (1680), a boy which is but upon his tenth year that does strange things in arithmetic. I remember when I was eight years old I learned the first declension without book. It did pain my tender brain, but perhaps it might have been the heat of the weather (in May) that caused my headache.

The seeds and sparks of virtue that lie buried in our souls unless actuated and cultivated by study and industry will certainly wither and vanish to nothing; but if encouraged by labour, they deeply spread and shoot up into maturity, and who knows not, that every man of his own nature and genius is prone and has a propensity to this or that? Mr. Ascham in his *Schoolmaster* says that a school should indeed be a house of play and pleasure and not of fear and bondage and so says Socrates in a place of Plato's *Republic*. Quintilian compares the memory of a child to a great bottle with a little neck or mouth into which you are to pour the licquor in gustations or else more will fall than enter in. Therefore let 'em learn but a little at a time; never above half an hour at grammar, but that perfectly, with interposition of bodily exercises suitable to their strength and age. And let them change studies; for example, from grammar to mathematics, from writing to graphics. The motto of Mr. Crumlam, schoolmaster of St. Paul's School is '*studiorum mutatio est laboris remissio*'. They should leave their studies with an appetite as they do their meals, or else they will hate and loathe their books and teaching. Fine, young, tender wits require inculcating: they are apprehensive enough, but not tenacious. Mr. Latimer, my first schoolmaster for a little while, who was schoolmaster to Mr. Hobbes at Malmesbury, was wont to give the lads a Latin word to remember every time they asked leave to go forth. There is a vocabulary of Westminster School in Latin and Greek and English, but that of Mr. John Ray is better, the words more correct.

Being now come to the Latin school, they are to go over to J. Comenius's *Ianua* again, first in Latin and next in Greek, and being acquainted with the matter, they will go through with more delight, for youths no longer than they are in pleasure are in pain, especially as to grammar learning, which after the common method is exceeding harsh. Their tender wits will turn like a razor—not so, an axe. By this method words and things will steal upon them insensibly: 'tis *stratum super stratum*, or as in limning, a thin and dilute colour and then another such thin coat on that, and so on until the colour is perfected. If you lay the colours on too thick and at one time they will crack and not hold their colour. So precepts are to be inculcated to children; and the most inventive are not generally the most tenacious.

Let them be taught to write by the method and invention of Israel Tonge, D.D.,[3] i.e., by a copy book printed with red ink, which copies the children are to trace over with a pen with black ink, and after a little practice to try now and then on a piece of paper. By this way the idea of the letters are so perfect in the child's fantasy that in twenty days' time practising two hours in the morning and two in the afternoon a child of nine years old will write a legible hand. These books are sold at the Coffee House in Finch Lane. Ludovicus Vives in his *Dialogues* teaches to write by clear directions. The Dutch method is that after they can form their letters they make them write with a text pen,[4] whereby, in great, the fault is more visible and they learn by this way to cut their letters better. And I would have their copies not nugatory or dry, insipid stuff, as usually, but mnemonic verses either of figures in rhetoric or mathematics; so, according to the adage *una fidelia duos dealbare parietes*. And they learn to write, let 'em learn to make figures, and to understand numeration; and then train them on to addition; and let them check the addition by adding backwards, which as Mr. Mercator says is the best way. And then, by degrees, let 'em make up the multiplication table themselves, after the method of N.

Mercator. It will please 'em to see by what easy and natural steps they do climb up to knowledge, and that it is now in their own powers to make such another, if lost. Everybody cannot go at the same pace; yet they may get to their journey's end. Mr. W. Oughtred was too quick for most of his scholars; *festina lente*. 'They who but slowly paced are, By plodding on may travel far', G. Withers [*Emblems*]; and Mr. Thomas Ax told me that his father taught him the table of multiplication when he was seven years old.

This school is, as before said, a *ludus literarius*. When the children do begin to speak Latin they will learn it apace. And when they come so far as the rule of three, they will learn mathematics as fast as the informator can instruct them, and they as willing to learn as he to instruct. The experience hereof I know by Dr. Newton's school at Ross in Herefordshire, by the mathematical boys of Christchurch Hospital and Mr. John Ward's private school.

To exercise and improve their memories let 'em read, for example in the first class, Ovid's *Metamorphoses* translated by Mr. G. Sandys in their respective classes a quarter or half an hour. For so little time they will be attentive, and then after a little, let them be called upon to rehearse what they can remember. It is incredible how much this way will improve their memories, which was the method used by the reverend and learned Edward Davenant of Gillingh, Dorset, D.D., to his children. By this means they could give a better account of a sermon than the boys of Winton School who took notes.

For the next superior class, one of them to read Sleidan, *de 4 Imperiis*, in English, which they are to rehearse as aforesaid, and then after they have read it in Latin they may read the Jesuits of the same subject, but better, printed at Oxford, which comes down to 1660. The next superior class to read Appian's *History* in English in like manner, before which time they are not capable to understand Cicero's *Epistles*. *Item*, Ld. Chancellor Bacon's *Essays*, Osborne's *Advice to his Son*, *The Art of Wheedling*, by ——, and *The London Jilt* or *The Politic Whore* all in like manner. And let them be told instances, how such and such men came to be ruined in their estates. This will make such a deep impression in their memories that they will never forget it, and cause them to have a love of learning, and after read the authors in Latin or Greek.

'It is best to begin with epitomes and afterwards good to end with them,' Theod. Bathurst, M.D. *Quare*, Sir [John] Hoskins of Sir Anthony Morgan's way of remembering what he had read (or perhaps heard rather than read, which is Mr. Edmund Waller's way, the poet) which was not by the a and b side of the leaf, but by the things themselves, as diagrams.

Let 'em never be idle; nay, let their every play be instructive. Let 'em always have in their pockets some dialogues, and Euclid's *Elements* as religiously a monk his breviary. Let 'em be told how to excerpe, for which purpose let every one have a little 12ᵐᵒ pocket book to enter excerps, either of reading or of observations either of men's knowledge, or *mores hominum, rerum naturalis,* poignant sayings or antiquities. This will create in them the habit of doing and continuing this way, and finding daily more and more use of it, they will continue it as long as they live. It was a considerable advantage to Sir Francis North, now Lord Keeper, besides his own good parts and excellence of wit, that his tutor (as his Lordship told me) made him properly to understand what he read to him before he left him, so no doubt was left upon him. Let this method be used through all the arts.

Whoso looketh into grammar schools may rightly wonder to see so little improvement of those worthy means this age enjoys. Many who take in hand to instruct youth require no exercise at all, or however, no way suitable to the books that are read in their schools. Others, exacting brick, but affording no straw, charging exercises upon their scholars yet neither showing how it may, nor (which is worse) observing that it be performed. Mr. Johnson's Preface to his *Scholar's Guide from the Accidence to the University* [1665].

Proverbs would be useful for them to learn and read and also set down in the Real Character which will fix it better in their minds.

The Italian proverbs are the better done into English, and I think the Spanish, which are the best. The best blood in the Spanish veins is derived from the Moors. The wisdom of a nation is much discerned by their proverbs and there is no nation so dull but have some sayings worth remembrance. There is a French grammar called the *French Alphabet* to which is annexed a *Treasury of the French Tongue,* wherein are all the French proverbs. Mr. Camden in his *Remains* has a collection of English proverbs, but Mr. John Ray has made a greater. Let these be sometimes read a quarter of an hour and repeated: it will mightily open understanding and their judgements.

These hints will be as *granum sinapis*—nest eggs. Their excerpts of observations in their note books will be repositories or stories from observations and experience, away beyond the common way of precepts as the knowledge of a traveller exceeds that which is gotten by a map. I know not where are to be found better specimens of this kind than in Ben Jonson's *Underwoods* which he calls ὕλη. He deeply read men and made his observations as he walked along the streets. Had he not done that, he had never wrote so well. He has outdone all men yet in dramatic poetry. Nature is the best guide and the best pattern: 'tis better to copy Nature than books, as the best painters imitate Nature, not copy it. This will put life and vigour into youths of ingenious spirits to see that by these steps the old writers came by their mastership. Drexilius inculcated *semper excerpe*. Then, as for notions which it shall please God to dart into their minds, those winged fugitives to be entered and so to become fixed, or otherwise, perhaps, they may be eternally lost.

Whilst invention is in the flux, let it run; for if it be checked 'tis like the stopping of a patient's breathing sweat, which is not easily regained. Let them exercise to make unpenned speeches, declamations or addresses. This way of exercise to the Lord Chancellor Bacon does much appear of all most useful. A Spanish Jesuit told a friend of mine that 'tis a good way, before one was to speak to a prince, or in a great assembly, to speak it first in one's chamber, to your bedpost, or to a picture. My Lord William Brereton, my honoured friend, told me he asked Dr. Burnet how he obtained that extraordinary mastership in preaching. The Doctor told him that when he began to be a preacher, he would go up into the mountains where he was sure nobody could hear him and speak aloud and by much practice he obtained this perfection.

Mr. J. Dryden in his Preface to *The Spanish Friar* says that description is the most principal part of poetry and deserves the greatest praise; in order to this, and to please their ingenious minds, let 'em read Mr. John Milton's *Paradise Lost* and *Paradise Regained*, as also the tales of Sir Geof. Chaucer which may be rightly called the pith and sinews of eloquence and very life itself of all mirth and pleasant writing. Besides, one gift he has above all other authors and that is by excellency of his descriptions, to possess his readers with a more forcible imagination of seeing (as it were) done before their eyes, which they read, than any other that ever has written in any other tongue.

These exercises of descriptions I would have in blank verse in English, or in prose (Latin or English for variety). At Westminster School they spoil their Latin proses by poetry and they think it such

57

a mighty matter for boys to make extemporary epigrams (jots and quibbles). I do not hear that they use this way. But the solving of a mathematical problem is worth a hundred epigrams.

They may, to refresh themselves, when they are tired with mathematical problems, read Ovid's *Metamorphoses* or Homer's *Iliad*, or those whose genius carried them on forcibly to be musicians, divertise themselves, when they begin to doze and false calculate, on the violin or chamber organ.

Read no book in English that they can in Latin (after they can speak Latin and understand it tolerably) to make themselves the more exact in the Latin language; which will be of great ornament to them on their travels beyond the sea: for they will hardly speak the foreign speech properly, but grate the natives' ears with their improprieties and ill-pronunciations, whereas they will love to hear 'em speak Latin so well, and 'twill gain them great reputation. And it might not be forgotten the great reputation that Cardinal Wolsey had when he was sent as envoy into France by King Henry VIII by speaking Latin so well. He could understand French, but when the French Cardinal spoke to him in French he made his return still in good Latin. (It was Cardinal Wolsey that made the accidence which is taught in our schools.)

The foreign ministers of state look on our ambassadors and envoys with scorn, not defective in this point, as ill-bred; or else not capable of learning.

In our schools the ways of study are desultory; from prose to verse one day, and the other, the other. Seek whether it would not be proper for them when they come to pretty good pass in their studies, to keep them a fortnight or so to logic and untying of fallacies: the like for ethics and the civil law, and for those that have a genius for poetry, to descriptions, as aforesaid. But more or less every day of the week they should exercise in algebra.[5]

Whereas it is objected that there is a natural and appointed time for wits to be ripe, namely, about sixteen, and that is they are not to be forced. 'Tis true that civil prudence comes by years, but mathematical prudence may be learned by boys and fine-forced, in order to which let there be drawn a list or catalogue of useful arithmetical questions for them to solve.

Now to exercise the memory which before was too tender and not well stuff't with shapes of things, their lessons should be short, not to overburden their memories.[6] Montaigne's advice is good, to decline verbs and nouns perfectly, and the syntax will come by use.

Mr. Christopher Wase has written an excellent short grammar of this method and there is a pamphlet called ——, printed 1660, which is a more compendious and clear way than has hitherto been attempted. After they are perfect in this scheme and the concords, and have learnt J. Am. Comenii *Ianuam* and played with the *Dialogues* of Corderius, namely by the way of constructing without a laborious repetition, for Latin is sooner gotten by rendering it into English than by forming English into Latin after the common fashion. A provost taught a gentleman's son to understand Latin quickly this way though he began methinks with an odd book for a youth, T—— *Offices* which he went over in a summer. The subject is too grave and unintelligible and unpleasant and the period tediously long.

Corderii *Dialogues* (as also Du Gres' *Dialogues*) are delicate Latin and adequate to the child's understanding: and when he begins a little to pick out the English, he will take such a delight in it, he will learn it very willingly. So they learn at first to swim with bladders.

A youth's way of learning should be *ludus literarius*, not a Bridewell. The globes I would have him play with so that he would understand them before he is aware: maps he will like well enough, too. Cluverius's *Geographie* is very easy Latin, which, by this time he will pick out; for the method must be from the most easy to the lesser; and last, to the old authors. The discipline of the schools being quite contrary hereunto, where first they jump into the most difficult that are. I have said before, I would have him taught arithmetic as soon as he can speak. Now the first thing he should commit to memory should be Oughtred's *Clavis*, the Latin whereof is easy, the rules incomparable: it is *magna in parvo*. That enchiridion containing more than Vieta's folio. By this means he will not only by a facile way leave Latin, climbing up step by step, but his arithmetic and rules will be so bred in the bone (as we may say) that it will be habitual and a great delight, ornament and use.

Let him be further introduced into geometry, and be *gradatim* and finally by twelve, perfect in it as his Paternoster.

Now he understands the Latin tongue pretty well, let him learn the grammar rules and read the classic authors, and let the first be the delightful poem, Ovid's *Metamorphoses*. Consider whether it would not be a good way to let him read it first in Mr. G. Sandys' translation, to make the better idea, and to draw him on with the greater delight. This poem should he always bear about him and have, as it were, by heart. So did the famous Dr. Collins of Cambridge, who could have repeated all the fine things of it: 'tis true he made himself master too of Cicero's *Attic Spirit*. But the other was his foundation and he was wont to confess to Mr. Robert Peyton, his schoolfellow, that by this way he came to his heights in oratory. Next, I would have him take into his hands the *Fairie Queen*: nowhere are better. Read Cooper's *Dictionary*; then Calepin's *Etymology*.

He may now, by the by, and insensibly, become more perfect in his astronomy from the globes. 'Tis not to be forgot that he will have perfectly in every gradation, his correspondent mnemonic verses (both in algebra and astronomy).

It exceeds belief to what perfection a boy of indifferent parts may be brought by this way. Ben Jonson in his $\nu\lambda\eta$ has an excellent treatise of education of a youth and he is utterly against breeding at home. But I would have him bred carefully at home in this method till twelve, and then sent to a public school (according to him) to be top'd and finished. That at Westminster is the best in England. 'Tis certain that at Westminster School some of his schoolfellows will become great men; a considerable advantage.

He will now be able to swim for his life, both for Latin and for arithmetic and geometry. When he can decline nouns and verbs in Greek, he should be put into the Greek Euclid, which is very easy; and understanding the propositions, he will shortly master it as well as Latin. So that this will not only draw on his Greek easily, but still keep up alive his geometry and arithmetic. By this time, or thirteen or fourteen, perfect in his algebra and arithmetic. It is to be noted that few are sent to great schools ill-grounded, understand not their grammar and to make true Latin, ever come to anything, but are neglected, and having brought an ill-foundation, despond; it is a rock on which many a good wit that I know has split. For the learning of grammar is the least care taken of at such schools. They learn there to be declaimators and poets, where emulation spurs one another forward, sometimes to admiration. But this is not all. It is now that he is entered to be of the world, to come from his innocent life, tender care, and indulgence of his parents, to be beaten by his schoolfellows, to be falsely accused, to be whipped by the master, to understand his tyranny and likewise the praepositor's. 'Tis here he begins to understand the world, the misery, falseness and deceitfulness of it: 'tis here he begins to understand himself, that he finds others to be his equals and superiors in honour, estate, wit and strength. Here he learns to make friendships which oft times continue as long as they live. Here he has a true copy for studying the passions; as likewise for physiognomy which will not fail when they are men, though then, through their cunning, they disguise it. This observation I have made myself; for they that were cheats then, are so still, or were so long as they lived— good-natured, good; bad, bad.

Mr. T. Hobbes' opinion to me was that he would not have a boy to make verses at fifteen or sixteen. But he himself, at fourteen, when he was old parson Latimer's scholar, translated Euripides' *Medea* into Latin iambics. (Inquire whether it were not better to enter them at thirteen to verses, that is to say, if they are sharp youths, ingenious and delight in poetry; otherwise let 'em prosodie alone, according to old Mr. Henley's advice, who spake like a wise man.) After he is well versed in Ovid and mythology let him read Virgil and Homer. Mr. Hobbes commends Catulus before Martial for the latter are jests in verse; the former is passions. Caesar's *Commentaries* and which he (Hobbes) made his pattern, and says it is in best Latin and style most courtlike. He would have a boy entered into geometry when he understands Latin, but that he is capable of before. The Greeks, no doubt, taught it to their children. It is the best way of teaching logic to Mr. Hobbes' way of thinking. It makes 'em reason without making a false step; it fixes their thoughts and cures bird wittedness; teaches to reason geometrically and analytically in other things, and consequently is an excellent preparative to the study of the laws. According to Mr. John Davenant, the most pertinent, and honourable and suitable study, and which gentlemen ought to understand. Therefore, I fear not the *ubi* of any dull justice, or grave burgher, that it will prejudice them to be so *ad omnia quare*.[7]

7

The Schools

I would have every class to be in several rooms. In the first school, for the novices, I would have several heads of illustrious men for empire, or arts, for local memories according to the method of Dr Tonge.

I would have several emblems well-painted to delight their ingenious young spirits with their mottoes selected proper for their fancy: they will both delight and instruct. For example:

A line drawn by a pen—*nulla dies sine linea.*

He that delights to plant and set
Makes after ages in his debt.

A spider persuing a fly—*Matura.*

A snail creeping—*festina lente.*

One with wings to his hands but a weight to his heels.
My wit got wings and high had flown,
But poverty doth keep me down.

The picture of the Horn of Suretyship.

Such they will remember when they come to be men, that this sentence was over such a one's head, and it may be of use to them in their conversation.

Quid de quoque viro et cui dicas saepe caveto   Horace, *lib.* I, *Epist.* 18.

The remembrance of this may save many of them from the Tower or from a duel.

In former times, as in some old houses is yet to be seen, which argues the goodness of that age, on the painted hangings were writ good, moral sentences. Sir Ralph Hopton, afterwards Lord, was wont to say that he learned more philosophy once from a painted cloth in an alehouse than in all the books he had read; *sc.*

> Never lament or make any moan,
> For either there's remedy, or there is none.

The provost's gallery should be near the schools with videttes to look in upon them undiscovered.

8

The Classes

Years of Age	Years at School	
10	1st	Decline nouns and verbs. Dr. Tonge's *Epitome* and Mr. J. Milton's tables in his *Accidence Commenc't Grammar* for genders of nouns and praeter perfect tenses and supines. Mr. Christopher Wase's *Praxis* and the rules of Emmanuel Alvarus's *Grammar*. The *Dialogues* of Corderius ('tis done into English).
11	2nd	I would not have them enter into Alvarus till 11 or more, but to continue their construing of dialogues, making grammar, and speaking Latin, their *Praxis* and their mathematics.
	2nd	Alvarus's *Grammar*, book 2, and peruse Walker's *Particles*. Ludovicus Vives' *Dialogues*. Du Gres' *Dialogues*. Ovid's *Metamorphoses* in English. Corderius's translation of some select epistles of Cicero. Greek grammar, and scan and turn verses.

64

12	3rd	Fr. Petrarch's *De Remediis utriusque Fortunae* which will furnish them with matter enough; and now they will be able to read Ovid's *Metamorphoses* in Latin with the help of Brinsley's translation. These two will furnish them with matter and similies for their *chrias*.
13	4th	Cicero's *Select Orations*. Appianus's *History*. Homer. Polybius's *Declamations and Descriptions*.
14	5th	Aristotle's *Ethics*. *Rudiments of the Civil Law*, towards the end of the year, namely *Disceptationes*. Quintilian's *Declamations*. Sanderson. *Euclid*, in syllogisms.
15	6th	Logic. Disputations. Zouch's *Elementa Juris Civilis*. Declamations.
16	7th	Aristotle's *Politics* and *Economics*. His *Logic* and *Physiognomy*. Disputations in civil law, politics and economics, and declamations.
17	8th	Travel in Germany first; Italy, second; France, third; England, fourth,
18	9th	*cum cursu chimiastico*, with a *continuando* of analytical learning.

By this method a youth of eighteen years of age will be a better grounded scholar, and more really learned than (generally) most of thirty or more.

Years of Age	Years at School	
10	1st	Writing and introduction to algorithms and graphics, globes. Show 'em constellations and plain trigonometry. (Let their nurses teach 'em to number about six years old.)
11	2nd	Continuation with arithmetic and begin with literal algebra and geometry, and when they have passed the first form, surveying, continued use of the globes, astrolabe, spherical trigonometry. Mr. Paschal's *Scheme* for Greek and Latin, and things in the Real Character.
12	3rd	Kersey's *Algebra*, together with Brancker's and Dr. Pell's *Questions* and Mr. Oughtred's *Clavis*. And a way of working, daily practising solving of questions. Practical mathematics; for example, perspective, architecture, fortifications, tactics.
13 14	4th	Still keeping up and continuing with algebraical exercises, but now beginning to improve as to the solution of questions or cases in the civil law. And so to proceed in that method to the common law, and to the solution of cases of conscience.

15	*Idem*
16	
17	
18	

Schoolmasters should be as prudent as grooms who part horses that fight and cannot agree and have an antipathy against each other. In like manner, if boys are not parted thus, they will mischief, maim or perhaps kill one another, which I have known.

9

School Exercises

To say over their grammars every six weeks, Latin in the morning, Greek in the afternoon. I would not have their *chrias*[1] which we call themes, esteemed by the length of them, but for the goodness of invention. Besides their *chrias* they are to declaim *pro* and *con.*; as also for and against offenders, where they will have recourse to the judicial, deliberative and demonstrative gender. Mr. R. Hooke says that declaiming is of no use, but only in the universities. But Sir Chr. Wren is of another opinion: he says that it makes them speak well in Parliament House.

The Jesuits do breed up their youth to oratory the best of any in the world. They have in their schools tribunes, dictators, *etc.*, and do exercise their oratory daily, both studied and *extempore*, so that they must of necessity be better orators than others not so bred.

It would be useful for them once in a week or fortnight, to *narrare* as in Trinity College, Oxford, at dinner and supper, standing at a screen, which I would have sometimes done in English. They are to pronounce clear and emphatically, to have a decent posture and action which, if they do not practise when they are young, they will never do either gracefully, as we frequently see in our parliament men how ungracefully they speak.

Therefore, I would have those that are come to make their *chrias* to be enjoined to contemplate and spin like the spider out their own bowels. This exercise will become delightful and habitual if they have any spark of celestial fire in them.

Of all—there is none deserves so much praise as description, which let be performed in blank verse in English, and sometimes in English prose to get them a good habit. There are descriptions by M. de Bergerac in 8º translated into English, better than the youths will probably make.

Let one read in Sleidan *de 4 Imperiis*, in English, half an hour, and the boys to give an account of what they can remember. This will wonderfully improve their memories and make them in love with history and chronology. And so they will be drawn to read it in Latin, which is a plain, proper and easy style. Let 'em read next *Flosculi Historici delibati; nunc delibatiores redditi auctore Jo. de Bussières de societate Jesu, editi tertia auctore et emendatior*, Oxon., 1668, very good Latin and succinctly done. He comes down to the restoration of King Charles II. How parents will wonder to hear little boys give a ready account of things from the beginning of the world to their times.

Once a week to read to the older youths half an hour out of Paul Barbett's *Praxis of Physic*, a little 8º, 2s. at Hen. Broome's. It is short, clear and useful, and teaches to check a distemper at the beginning. I have heard the learned Dr. Ridgeley, M.D., say that if the world knew the villainy and knavery of the physicians and apothecaries the people would throw stones at 'em as they walked in the streets.

To read half an hour distinctly Mr. Osborne's *Advice to his Son*, and the young gentlemen to make a rehearsal. The like for the *Art of Wheadling* to give them a true and lively account of the gamesters, cheats, menspoyles (the greatest pest upon the earth), spongers and hangers-on, of flatterers, of tailors and tradesmen, cheats of young heirs; of Mr. Dutton's cheat to the Earl of Carnarvon by cutting and sewing the stirrup, for example.

At every meal, let 'em learn a mnemonic verse or some good sentence—the Druids delivered their learning in mnemonic verses—which in time will be a considerable advantage. Let them, like pretty bees, be always excerping, which in time will be a considerable advantage. *Semper excerpe*, in some kind or other. One may take a hint from an old woman or a simple body. Contemn nobody; aim still at truth. Had I not excerped these notions that are here stitch't together, and good part whereof I got from my learned friend Dr. Jo. Pell, had been utterly lost and buried in oblivion.

Let 'em analyse a proverb; for example, as Dr. Sanderson has done INVIDIA in his appendix of his *Logic*.

What if they did read Pliny's *Natural History?* 'Tis excellent Latin, pleasant and instructive. Also Maffei's *Historia* and his *Epistles* and Pliny's *Epistles*—admirable and delightful.

The young ladies in London do learn as far as the rule of three and the rule of practice, and do find it to be a great use to them in buying of their silks, laces, *etc.*, but this belongs rather to a *gynaeceum*.

Mr. Ri. Yeomans, a schoolmaster of mine, was wont to say that invention did run highest about the age of twenty three. Colerus, a German, in his *Book of Agriculture* says that they do every morning tell their dreams, and that they do find it significant and useful. Also, let those (or the most innocent and angelical, virtuous youths) look into berills or crystals.

Solemn and Festival Exercises

I would have the solstices and equinoxes observed in the nature of holidays, but mixing with their jolity, arithmetical observations of the sun.

Also, being Christians, we should remember with Holy Church the 16th December, *sc.*, *O Sapientia*. I would have the annual *Encomia* comemmorated with the usefulness of the institution, and orations made.

Exercises for Sundays and Holydays

I would not have them go to the parish church: they would be gaping about and pick up acquaintance. After morning prayer, one to read distinctly for half an hour out of the *Whole Duty of Man*, on which they are to ruminate and give an account *memoriter* before dinner. After evening service, or before, to construe the Gospel in Latin or Greek, according to their station. (First and second class.)

After morning prayer is ended, let one read distinctly for half an hour, one of Dr. Sanderson's sermons, Dr. Tillotson's or Mr. Tombs' *Shephansheba*: of the which before dinner or before evening service, they are to render what account they can, *memoriter*, which will meliorate their memories and their judgements. After dinner, let 'em read Dr. Tho. Aquinatis *Secunda Secundae*. (Third and fourth class.)

And as grammars are made out of classical authors, so let 'em exercise to make a kind of theology of their own, out of their observations of God's wonderful works, of his miraculous preservation; of some persons, of their own particular deliverance from dangers.

10

The Library

I would have belonging to this school a good library of well-chosen books, such as are useful to the young gentlemen; or that may be within their virtue to make 'em acquainted with good authors and so to fall in love with books, which is a good step to being learned. But I would have this library ordered with this restriction, that they should never be in the informator's possession: nay, not the provost's. And once a year, an inspection to be taken of them; for example, the first Monday after Michaelmas day. And a duplicate to be left with the Lord Lieutenant of the county to prevent embezzelling, which is many times done by the schoolmaster (for example, at Blandford); or some other peer that has a house nearby; (for example, for the school at Merton, the Earl of Pembroke's house at Wilton), where in case of war or such extraordinary calamity the books and the instruments would carefully be conferred.

Emmanuel Alvarus, *Grammatica.*

J. Amos Comenius, *Vestibulum Novissimum Latinae Linguae*, London, 1647.
Didactica Opera; ubi lemmata de educatione. In folio.

Dr. Vossius (the son says he accounts his father's *Grammar* the best; John Gerard Vossius.

Mr. Farnaby's *Grammar.*

Walker's *Particles. Phrases.*

Mr. Christopher Wase's *Praxis.*

Mr. John Milton's *Grammar*, 8º, 6 sheets.

Mr. Dugres, his French Grammar, very clear and short.

Cleonard's Greek Grammar.

An English Introduction to the Latin Tongue for the use of Westminster School, 1659.

Schickard's *Horologium Hebraecum*, which will serve this turn.

Mr. S's Printed table (one sheet) of the Hebrew roots.

Ben Jonson's *Works*, in which is his English grammar.

W. Holder, D.D., *Elements of Speech.*

Statuta immunitates et jurisdictiones forma a Cels. Pr. Auriaco, Rectori, Professori et Studiosis Illustris Scholas in Urbe Bredae, 1646.

Inauguratio Illustris Scholae ac Illustt, Colleg. Auriaci a Cels. Principe Frederico Henrico in Urbe Bredae erectorum Breda MDCXLVII.

Vigerius, *de Particulis Linguae Graecae.*

Drexilius, *Aurifodina.*

Mr. Ascham's *Grammar.* I could never see it.

Laurentius Valla.

Brinsley's *Grammar School,* 1612, 4ᵗᵒ, at Mr. Hussey's in Little Britain. Dr. Pell says it is a good book.

Mr. Mulcaster's *Grammar School.*

M. T. Cicero, his *Works.* Hamburgh edition is the best, says Dr. Vossius. *Orations,* with Frigus's notes. 3 vols.

J. Caesar's *Commentaries.*

Terence, Englished by Brinsley, 1607, in 4ᵗᵒ.

Plautus, with the notes of Janus Dousa.

Vareny's *Geographia* would be delightful and useful to them and also it is pocketable.

Ovid's *Works,* with notes of Bersmannus in folio. The Dauphin edition is the best.

G. Sandy's translation of his *Metamorphoses*.

Virgil, with notes by Servius.

Homer's *Works*, with Dydimus his notes, and Eastathius's notes and John Ogilby's. Mr. Hobbes' translation and Chapman's.

Sir Geoffrey Chaucer.

Spenser's poems.

Milton's *Paradise* and his *Familiar Letters*.

The Greek minor poets.

A. Gellius, *Noctes Atticae*.

Quintilian.

Baudii, *Epistola*.

Dr. Pell commends Cleonard's *Epistles* (that made the Greek grammar).

Mr. Edmund Waller commends Annibal Caro, in Italian, 4to, as the most natural and useful, *qd. N.B.*

Maffei, *Epistola*; very good Latin.

Dictionaries

Calepin's *Dictionaria Mathematica*.

Martinus Martinius, *Dictionaria Geographica*.

Cooper.

Holyoke.

Florio's *Italian Dictionary*.

Cotgrave's *Dictionary*.

J. Gerard Vossius's *Lexicon*.

J. Comenius, *Lexicon Januale; hoc est Latinae Linguae sylva vocum derivitarum copiam explicans*. MDCL.

Spelman's *Glossary*.

Weclock's *Saxon Dictionary.*

Stephen's *Thesaurus.*

Scapuleius's *Lexicon.*

Calvinius's *Dictionary.*

Welsh dictionary.

High and Low Dutch dictionaries.

Agriculture

Columella and *Varro*, by Henry Stephanus.

Baptista Porta's *Villa*; an excellent book, 4to.

Markham.

La Maison Rustique [Stephanus, Charles Estienne].

Colerus, in High Dutch; a folio.

Systema Agricultura, by J. Worbiels of Hampshire.

Mr. Theodore Haak tells me that——a German baron, has writ the best of any one.

Mr. Yarrington's *Improvements.*

Constantini, *Geoponica.*

Biblia

St. Hierom's Bible; of the old, black print, by which they will learn to read manuscripts and records.

Biblia, das ist, die gantze Heilige Schrifft Deudsch. Martin Luther; printed at Bremen. It is written in the Saxon dialect, which is the best dialect of Germany. This book will open to them a way for the understanding of the old Saxon laws and the old English; and etymologies (J. Pell).

The new edition of Elhardus Lubinus's *New Testament*, Latin and High Dutch interlinery, 1614. Of excellent use for learning the German language.

Logic

Aristotle's *Organon* with the notes of Alexander Aphrodisaeus. But also all Aristotle's works.

Dr. Sanderson's *Logic* is the best of an epitome.

Burgherdicius's *Logica*.

Case's *Logic*. 'Tis out of fashion, but he writes very plain.

Cicero's *Orations* in three volumes with notes of Frigus, in 8⁰ for Sir Charles Scarborough: it shows the logic of it.

Suarez' *Metaphysics*; most of the school divinity is in it.

Blunderville has in print a logic in English in 4⁰, which is very plain and full of examples. I do fancy it is a useful book, though it is not taken notice of by any universities.

The Logician's Schoolmaster; a comment upon Ramus, his logic, by Mr. Alexander Richardson, sometimes of Queen's College in Cambridge, London; 1629, 4⁰.

Histories

T. Livy, with notes by Varro; Polybius in folio; Appianus in folio; Lucius Florus, with notes by Sandys; Cornelius Tacitus, with notes by J. Lipsy.

William of Malmesbury.

John Speed's *Chronicles*.

Helvicius's *Chronology*.

Isaacson's *Chronology*.

Nova Legenda Angliae, J. Capgrave.

John Magnus, *Historia Gothorum.*

Rerum Normanniarii Scriptores.

Harpsfield, *Historia Angliae.*

Mariana, *de rebus Hispaniae.*

Maffei, *Historia Indica.*

Arithmetic

Hylles's *Arithmetic,* 4º, 1600; where are some excellent mnemonic verses.

Boethius's *Works,* especially for his arithmetic, music and geometry.

Diophantus, with notes by Casp. Bachet. Paris; folio.

Michael Stiphelius's *Arithmetic.* 4º.

Syntaxis Mathematica, 8º, by Thomas Gilsen; a pretty analytical treatise.

Simon Stevinus de Bruges, *Works.*

Mr. Thomas Harriot's *Algebra.*

Vieta's *Works.*

William Oughtred's *Works.*

Briggs' *Logarithms.*

Vlack's *Logarithms,* folio.

Wingate's *Arithmetic.*

Dr. John Pell's *Table of* 10,000 *quadrates.*

Kersey's *Algebra* and *Geometry.*

Arithmetical Questions, touching the buying and exchange of annuities, taking of leases, for fines, or yearly rents, purchase or fee-simple. Dealing, for present and future possession, by R. W., London, 1613.

James Peele, *Merchant's Accounts.*

John Collins, *An Introduction to Merchant's Accounts*, folio, 1674

Robert Vernon's, *The Complete Counting House.*

Sir Jonas More's *Systema*, 2 vols.

Tables of Leases and Interest and their Grounds, in four tables of fractions, Anonymous, London, 1628, 8°.

The Merchants' Mirror, translated out of the Dutch into English at the end of *Lex Mercatoria*. John Collins in his *Account Book*, 1653, says it may serve as an appendix to *The Merchants' Mirror. The Stile of Exchanges, containing both their laws, customs, unfolding their mysterie.* Translated out of the Dutch, French and Latin, 8°. sold by —— Bringhurst in Gracechurch Street, 1682.

Le Thieser de Tenir Liure des Accompts, par H. Wanningen, imprimé à Amsterdam, 1648.

Advice concerning Bills of Exchange, by John Marius, Public Notary. London, by N. Bourne, 1655.

Chordarum Arcubus Circuli primariis ... authore Adriano Romano Equite, Comite Palatino et Medico Caesareo. Wircheburghi, A.D. 1602. Very rare: a thin, long folio an inch thick. I believe there is no other in England but Dr. Pell's.

Geometry

Archimedes' *Works.*

Euclid's *Works* in Greek.

Item, with Clavius's commentaries.

Item, with Billingsley's commentaries, and Dee's.

Item, Sir Henry Savile's edition and his lectures in 4°.

Barrow's *Euclid.*

de Chales' *Euclid.*

Fournier on the first six books; also Greenbergerus.

Herigon's *Cursus Mathematicus.*

Appolinarius's *Conics.*

Mydorgius's *Conics.*

Les Coniqs de Monsieur de la Hier.

Mr. Baker's *Conics.*

John Pell, D.D., *Works.*

A Treatise of the Combinations, Elections, Permutations, Compositions of Quantity, by Thomas Strode, Gent. London, 1678; 4° sticht.

The Way to Measure and Survey Timber by Tables, by —— of Sherborne, in Dorsetshire, near 100 years since. (Ask H. Coley for it.)

Wing's *Surveyor.*

Leybourn's *Surveyor.*

Holwels' *Surveyor.*

Thomas Digges *Stratioticos*, which I have, which Dr. Pell did me the favour to peruse, and has solved the questions there, after his own way, which I have annexed to the book now in the Museum at Oxford.

Dr. Isaac Barrow's *Archimedes* and *Apollinarius's Conics.*

Common Law

Littleton's *Tenures.*

Sir Edward Coke upon them; all his works.

The old *Registrum Brevium.*

Fitzherbert's *Abridgement.*

Judge Herbert's *Reports.*

Judge Rolle's *Commentaries.*

Mr. Plowden's *Commentaries.*

The Lawyers Light, by Judge Doderidge, where he puts the law arguments into syllogisms. A thin 4to.

Mr. Wingate's *Abridgement of Statutes.*

Finch's *Lawe.*

March's *Actions for Slander, and Arbitrement,* 1674.

Politics

Aristotle's *Politics,* with —— notes; as also his *Economics.* The Duke of Rosne has writ a comment on Aristotle's *Politics* in French, according to modern instances or examples: a very good book, wherein he shows by instances of succeeding times that all Aristotle's rules are infallible.

Dr. Case's *Politics* is said to be the best book he wrote and very good for a young man to peruse.

Meditationes Politicae . . . Politica Parallela XXV Disputationibus ante hoc exposuit. J. Christ. Becmannus, LL.D., ed. 3rd, Francofurti, 1677.

Thomas Hobbes' *Leviathan.*

Oceana, James Harrington.

The Latin volumes of the *Republic.*

Civil Law

Disputiones ad Instituta Imperialia, by Jacob Wisenbachius, 3rd edition 4to, printed at Leiden, 1676; the clearest book to begin withall.

Dr. —— Zouch, LL.D., *Elementa Juris Civilis; De Jure Feudali; Jus Feciale; De Judice Competente; Questiones Juris Civilis Centuaria,* the 2nd edition, 1682. (Get whatever he wrote.)

William Grotius, *De Principiis Juris Civilis.*

Vinnius, *De Origine Juris.*

Samuel Pufendorf, *Elementa Jurisprudentia Universalis*, lib.ii, cum Appendice de Sphaera Morali et Indicibus. Cantabrig. 1672.

Samuel Pufendorf, *De Jure Naturae et Gentium.*

Paraphrase des Institutions de L'Empereur Justinian, contenant une claire explication du texte Latine, avec beaucoup de réflexions morales et politiques, par Monsieur Pelisson, à Paris 1684.

Imperatoris Justiniani Institutionum, lib.iv, quibus adiuncti leges xii, tabb. explic., Ulpiani, tit.xix adnotat.

Caii, lib.ii, *Instituta,* Amsterdam, 1642.

Gotofredus upon the Institutes.

Vinnius upon the Institutes.

Minsinger upon the Institutes.

De Origine, et Progressa Juris Civilis Romani Auctoris et de Origine Juris. Leiden, 1672.

Reae Speculi, per . . . Duranti; a great folio in bibliotheca R.S., ubi in initio de jure et lege; an old print.

Julius Pacii, *Epitome Juris,* and his *Works.*

Constantine Hermanopulus, *Judicis Thessaloniensis Promptuarium.*

Ethics

Aristotle's *Ethics.*

Case's *Ethics.* The disputation part is very plain and easy to introduce beginners.

Secunda Secundae, Th. Aquinatis.

Cicero's *Offices.*

P. Charron's *de la Sagesse.*

Lord Bacon's *Essays* and got with it three several editions to see how he did improve. 'Tis as considerable an instance of this kind as is to be shown.

Senhault's *Of the Passions. Item,* de Jaranento.

Shephersheba, or the Oath-Book; being cases of conscience, by——Tombs, B.D., printed by Andrew Crooke, 1661. 4to, stich't.

Dr. Sanderson's *Sermons. Item,* de Jaranento.

Miscellaneous

All my Lord Chancellor Bacon's writings.

All des Cartes.

The Real Character, by J. Wilkins, Lord Bishop of Chester.

Mr. Hooke's *Micrographie;* 'twill mightily delight the boys.

J. Meursius, e Soc. Jesu, *de Luxu Romanorum,* which Sir Leoline Jenkins tells me is better than Bullinger.

Euclid's Physicus and *Metaphysicus,* by Thomas White, (Albio), 1657, 1658.

Baccius, *de Vinis,* which Dr. Plott says is the best.

Hieronymus Mercurialis's *de Re Gymnastica.*

Proverbs, collected by James Howell, Esq., *sc.* English, Italian, Spanish, British, in thin folio, 1659.

Molines' *Lex Mercatoria:* the last edition, 1685; the first was 1622. Where amongst several excellent discourses are good remarks of mines.

Grammar, Laurentius Valla.

Natural philosophy. Newton's *Principia Mathematica,* Trinity College, Cambridge, 1687, 4to.

An Essay of Human Understanding, by John Locke.

Juris Civilis . . . redditum per J. Meruram[?], Lugduni, 1556.

Leon Lessius, *De Justitia et Jure.*

Hugo Grotius, *De Jure Belli et Pacis;* in this, *Observationes Politicae et Morales,* Henricii Henniges, Salisbachii, 1673.

Feudales Controversia undecem disputationibus, à Sigismund Finckel-thauss, Lipsiae, 1630.

—— Haegmaierus, *De Jure Feudali.*

Caspar Zeigleri, *De Juribus Majestatis Tractatus Academicus*, Wittemburga, 1681. 'Tis an excellent book and good lemmata. There is an historical proceeding of a law-suit from the beginning to the ending, in Dutch: very pretty and useful.

Mr. Thomas Hobbes of Malmesbury, *De Legibus* which is printed at the end of his *Rhetorique.*

George Feltmanus, *De Feudis*—the best; better than Zouch.

Marsellaer, *De Legatis*, in 4to, Fabian Philipps says it is a very good book for the instruction of embassadors.

Processus Juris Brevissimis Versibus, redditus a Sebastiano Sheffero, Aldenberghensi Francofurti, 1572, in octavo.

Sharrock, *De Finibus et Officiis.*

Codex Legum Antiquarum, ex bibliotheca . . . Lindenburgi: a great folio, printed about 1600. Fabian Philipps says that Sir Henry Spelman made great use of it.

Medicine

—— Ettmullerus.

—— Wertzung in English; 'tis a good old book.

Astrology

Ptolemy's *Quadripartite* (if it be his).

Origen's *Astrology.*

Leovitius, *Introductio ad Astrologiam*, 4to; most methodical and short.

Leovitius, *de Conjunctionibus Magnis*, where he shows the effects of history from the time of Julius Caesar to Maximilian, the Emperor.

Stoffler's *Astrolabe*, at Mr. Lees', the globemaker in the Vinery, with the book of the use of it which children will much delight in.

Geography and Navigation

Chevorii, *Geographia.*

Ptolemei, *Geographia.*

Varenii, *Geographia Universalis.*

Jonston's *Geographia Vetus*, folio.

Blaeu's Maps and Speed's Maps.

Mr. —— Newton's *Navigation.*

Seller's *Art of Navigation.*

Norwood's *Art of Navigation.*

Wright's *Errors of Navigation.*

Herbals

Tabernaemontanus.

Parkinson's.

Gerard's.

Lovell's.

Mr. John Ray's *Works.*

Simeon Pauli, a Dane, *Quadripartit Botanicum.*

Chemistry

Andreas Libarius, *Of Mines and Minerals*, 4to, 1597.

Scroderi, *Pharmacopoeia.*

Georgius Agricola, *de Rebus Metallicis.*

Mechanics

Dr. Wilkins' *Mathematical Magic.*

The French manuscript of mechanics; an excellent piece, 4 or 5 sheets. N. Mercator and Captain Wyld.

Schottus's *Mechanics.*

Guido Ubaldus ——, a Jesuit.

Mr. Moxon's *Mechanical Exercises.* Choice collection of prints of this nature.

Salomon de Caus.

The best authors of perspective.

Astronomy

Ptolomy, in Greek.

The Description and Use of the Planetary System; together with easy tables by which the apparent motions of the heavens may be readily found for ever, by Thomas Street, 1674. Sold by Robert Morden at the Atlas in Cornhill.

John Kepler's *Works.*

Mr. N. Mercator's *Epitome of Astronomy.*

Mr. Street's *Astronomia Carolina.*

Mr. Edmund Halley's *Astronomy.*

Mr. Mercator's *Astronomy,* in 8°; note i.e. by Kauffman.

The Use of the Planisphere, called the Analemma, by John Twysden, M.D., 4 sheets, sold by Mr. Hayes at the Cross Daggers in Moorfields.

To which add *L'Usage de la Sphere Plate Universelle, avec son explication,* 4to, 65 pages, à Rouen, 1650. Let it be translated.

Stoffler's *Astrolabe*—this will be as much as youth can desire. To which I would have Henry Coley add the 2nd and 3rd problem out of —— Deusu.

Astrolabii Compendium auctore John Martino, 8°, Lutetia, 1557, with Mr. Lamb.

Mathematical Instruments

Besides the necessary instruments that every scholar is to have of his own, as: scale, compasses, sector, protractor and globes, I would have an apparatus of standing instruments for the school. For example:

Mr. Oughtred's Great Circles of Proportion, near a yard in diameter.

The Common Globes, and that of the Earl of Castlemain's. Also that of Copernicus.

Mr. Street's Planetary Instrument.

Maps and sea-charts. Projections of the sphere. Seiges of Maestricht, Breda, Candia, Vienna, *etc.*, and fortifications, Ptolemy's Analemma. Blagrave's Mathematical Jewel. Stoffler's Astrolabe. Jacob's Staff. Gunter's Quadrant and a sinicall quadrant for taking heights of towers. A theodelite; a circumferentor. Plain-table. A little cross-staff invented by Mr. Fuller that one may carry in his pocket; very useful for surveying.

Mr. Spiedell's *Rules for Measuring Timber.*

A circle divided into 360 degrees, within a rate and a ruler, by Ralph Greatrex, for trigonometry. E[dmund] W[yld] Esq., has one pasted on a board.

Sir Jonas Moore's Instrument that he made for his Royal Highness the Duke of York when he went to sea, mentioned in his *Compendium.* Captain Wynd has it in paper.

The Arithmetical Engine invented by Jeremiah Grinken.

Mr. Nich. Mercator's Ruler which serves for navigation, for directions in astrology, and by it one may calculate an eclipse. Mr. Joel, the mathematical instrument maker by Fleet-bridge, made it.

Parson Craddock of ——, in Suffolk, that painted so rarely after the dead life, had a parallelogram ten or twelve feet long.

Mr. Robert Hooke, R.S.S., invented a useful portable instrument for surveying which is not above four or five inches long, armed with a little telescope which will do to great exactness. Mr. Pitfield has one.

Let 'em be furnished with microscopes, telescopes, dark-room for taking one's picture, or landscape; it will set them agog, as they say.

In the Library I would have cabinets or drawers for repositories for minerals and another for samples of drugs.

By the time that boys are eighteen years old, or sooner, 'tis easy to find to what kind of learning their geniuses do lead 'em. This cannot be discovered at the common schools where they are kept to versifying till that age. See *Examen di Ingenioni*, translated out of the Spanish into English. It is a great advantage to find out a boy's genius. Cicero says in *lib.* I, *Offic.*, '*ad quas ergo res aptissimi erimus, in iis potissimum elaborabimus*,' and in another place he says, '*Suum quisque noscat ingenium*'. Some boys are so overfull of spirit that they will never endure the tedious process of our common schools, though they have good wits. Such may probably learn Latin after this natural and easy way, and may make good mathematicians or mechanics or chemists.

A few books, but well chosen, thoroughly digested with constant practice and observation, does the business. Mr. Hobbes and Mr. William Petty have several times confessed to me that had they read only as much as other men, they should have known no more than other men: neither are Sir Ch. W[ren] or Mr. R. H[ooke] great readers.

Somebody says to this purpose, '*non minor est pars scientiae cognitio quorum librorum*'. When I was a gentleman commoner at Trinity College, Oxford, 'twas my great happiness to have the friendship of the learned Mr. Ralph Bathurst, A. M. (now Dean of Wells). He had an excellent collection of well chosen books of all kinds of learning, and I still do owe my thanks to him for his generous favour to let me turn them over and peruse them. This made me fall in love with books. The currish Fellows would not suffer their pupils to do it; like ill-masters of trades that take good sums of money with their apprentices and never disclose to them the mystery of their trade. So much does a gentleman differ from a clown. Now without such a generous friend's manuduction, though a young man understand Latin and Greek well, and has a mind to learning and money to spare to buy books when he comes to Paul's churchyard, or the like, he finds mountains of books, but knows not with whom to begin and whom to peruse next, and, *deinceps*, who lead him into the way, who parologises and amuses him, for they all are bound alike. To obviate which inconvenience, and as an allurement to young men that have a mind to knowledge, and to be freed from the rust and mouldiness of ignorance, *exempli gratia* like a nomenclature of books only, I have put down a catalogue of some few for a library for such a school, which in a short time would be furnished with such, or a better collection: as also of mathematical instruments. This library will bring them acquainted with good authors and make them in love with books.

As for history, it is a large field and too long a work for this cursus, and too sour for their sweet relish; but hereafter, when they have the leisure and an inclination to it, that they may not be without a manu-duction, let them have Mr. Degore Wheare's *Relectiones Hyemales* where are the best directions for this kind of study. *Instructions for History, with a character of the most considerable historians ancient and modern,* out of the French, translated by Mr. John Davys of Kydwelly. These are good directions, but I believe the former is much better. Mr. William Prynne's advice to me for the reading of an English history was to read the authors that wrote of their own times.

The knowledge of things past is pleasing and necessary—good instruction for those that shall come hereafter, showing us the means, advice and policies whereby we may produce grace, help, comfort, or *a contra*. All of which are of great consequence to a man, as well for his private affairs as his public. Polybius, *lib.* III.

Grammar*

In his *Learning the Latin Tongue*, translated by Mr. Sam. Hartlib and dedicated to the then parliament, Elhardus Lubinus, complaining of the common and tedious method of teaching the Latin tongue says that it would induce one to think that some evil daemon had put it into the head of some monks to make grammar obscure and tedious, and to be learning six or seven years and not be able to speak it. And with whips and blows and gehennas, to make little boys hate learning.[1] To take off them, and obviate this old-fashioned monkish method of teaching tyrannically, first according to Mr. Montaigne's, let the boys learn to decline nouns and conjugate verbs, and the syntax will come by use. And as for a short and clear prospect of grammar, let them first learn Dr. Israel Tonge's in two half sheets here adjoined.

Eight Parts, two numbers, six Cases these,
Three Genders, Five Declensions, three Degrees,
Nineteen Pronouns, four kinds of Verbs, and they,
Three Persons, through two Numbers do convey.
Four Conjugations perfect verbs receive,
On which four Moods attend, and Tenses five,
From race of verbs, four Participles flowe,
Three Gerunds we admit, and Supines two.
These things well-laid, three Concords rise at last;
A structure: and the toil of grammar's past.
Noun-substantives, the names of things declare,
And adjectives, what kind of things these are.

* See also Appendix C.

One is the number Singular; but all
Above one, we the Plural number call,
The Nom'native before the verb doth goe,
Of shows the Genative: the Dative to.
Th'Accusative after the verb is plac't.
The fifth calls: Praepositions rule the last.[2]

It is much after the method of Christopher Wase's *Praxis*. About 1670, he taught scholars at the house of Sir —— Fisher at Islington in Middlesex [see p. 162]. His school was in the gallery, where he pinned up several prints; for example, the heads of Alexander the Great, Julius Caesar, Hannibal, Scipio, Aristotle, Archimedes, *etc*. Verbs governing such and such were wrote down in a scroll or catalogue under such and such a hero's head, so that when they came to a verb that governed an ablative case, it presently occur'd to their memories, Oh, this verb is under Julius Ceasar's head, and *sic de cetoris*, which way of local memory made a fast impression or Idea in their tender memories; so that the boys did make a grammar themselves as they read their authors. By setting down under the respective heads, the examples they met withall in classical authors, which yet made the impression deeper in their memories.

He made them to learn Latin words every day, as also Greek, and taught them to construe in the Latin or Greek Testament thus. After a little practice, he would make them to write out the words of a page, or half a page, that they had not learned before, and English them (or, if Greek, in Latin), which, having learnt, they would construe these verses of the chapter in the Gospel with great facility; and they took a great delight in it. Nay, I heard these two or three young gentlemen construe some of the Gospel there. Besides this, he did exercise them to speak Latin. When they were got beyond the *Praecepta XXI Gramatica* Em. Alvari, they did learn their Latin and Greek together, which he said was the best way, for that they were so near akin.[3]

Let them learn the *XXI Praecepta de Constructione* (translated into English) *Institionum Linguae Latinae*, Emanualis Alvari, with which let them use Mr. Chr. Wase's *Praxis*. Let them use double translation; namely to translate out of the Latin into English and then turn that English into Latin again. And this is the best and quickest way (says Mr. Roger Ascham, who taught Queen Elizabeth after this manner) of learning any language. After Mr. Wase's *Praxis*, and Mr. Ascham's way, let them practise to turn English into Latin by the guidance of

Mr. Walker's excellent book of *Particles*. Let them be so much the masters of Walker's *Particles* as that they are able readily to give either the English for the Latin or Latin for the English.

The utility of it is great, for there can be no speaking or writing Latin with any assurance of the propriety of the language without some competent skill in these Particles; the want of which is the cause of the most of these barbarisms committed in writing and speaking by young learners. Walker's *Particles*.

Directions for the better learning of the Latin tongue, Anon.:

that in the common schools they do go preposterously to work, that make Latin first, or at least their chief exercises for their scholars themes and verses, which require elegancy as well as propriety. Whereas they should at first exercise them well in plain and proper style, by making epistles and dialogues, or telling stories or making relations; by which they will learn to speak purely and properly upon any subject. When they can do that, elegancy of speech will come itself, being a thing that depends upon fancy and invention.

Let them read and double translate Cicero's *Oratorium Selectarum Liber, editus in usum scholarum Holandiae et Westphaliae ex decreto J. H'mont, D.D., ordinum eiusdem provinciae*, whereunto is annexed Matthei Natheni *Observationes Analytica*, Amsterdam, 1659. I would have 'em to learn some of these by heart, and to pronounce them emphatically. This way will teach them to invent, and will let them know all these fine things did not drop from his pen at once, or were not done, as they say, at one heat. That the notions came into his thoughts at several times, and that at last, he digested them into this excellent order.[4]

Let them write down the lemmata or arguments of an oration, and then cut them to pieces with a pair of scissors, and shuffle them and let the boys put them in as good order and method as they can; and let the rhetoric master instruct them and show them where right, where wrong. The like I would have 'em to practise with the arguments of Monsieur Balzac's *Roman, Maecenas, etc*; cut out as aforesaid and then to put them in as good order as they can, in English, or in Latin. The rhetorication of Balzac is more *à la mode* and juvenile, and more agreeable to the genius of youths than the gravity and prudence of the judicious consul. Hereafter, let 'em peruse the *Analysis of Persius* by —— Lambinus.

Teach 'em to make their *chrias* analytically in imitation of the aforesaid samples, and let them use themselves to write clearly. Let them read Baudii *Epistola* and the *Epistles* of Peter Maffei: as also his *Historia Indica* which is delicate Latin, and the style easy and the subject much more delightful than that of any old classic author. Mr. Edmund Waller, the poet, much commends Fr. Petrarch *de Remediis Utriusque Fortunae* as very fit for boys, where they will be furnished with a variety of matter. Mr. Thomas Cooper, in his *Dictionary*, of Appianus says thus: 'He was a noble historian, born in Alexandria, wrote most excellent works of the Roman Civil Wars, which books I counsel all them that be studious in Tully's works to read diligently, whereby they shall understand many things that else they cannot well understand.' After they are well-versed in this useful and delightful author they will be able to understand Cicero's *Epistles* and the rest of his works. Caesar's *Commentaries* would be a book now proper for them to read.[5] But I would have one of the boys should read a leaf at a time, once or twice a day, of Appian in English, to which all that class is to be attentive, and then after a little time of recollecting, to give an account of what they heard read. This is the best and most useful way of improving boys' memories, and they will vie one with another, through emulation, who can remember most.

This way of exercising the memories is much better than the way commonly used in our grammar schools where they jade the boys' memories with learning memoriter all their lessons out of the classic authors, which is tiresome to youths as not carrying delight along with it; for boys no longer than in pleasure are in pain. This method the Reverend Ed. Davenant of Gillingh, D.D., used in the education of his sons, as also for sermons, which he accounted better than for them to take notes in writing as the common fashion was. I believe he that writes does not remember so well as he that gives attention and does not write.

When they are about twenty or more, I would have them read Livy, and it may not be beneath 'em sometimes to consult the translation of Philemon Holland, who understands it perfectly well. Besides the greatness of the subject, 'tis excellent Latin and style. Terence and Plautus I would have them read, but I am not now of the opinion that they are so useful and fit to imitate as is commonly thought. The Latin is very good for that purpose for drama, which is practical, but not proper to be used in prose. Sir Henry Wotton says somewhere, jestingly, that verse is the best way of writing next to prose, and it is certain that too much reading of the poets spoils a good prose style. For which reason I would have them meddle as little with the poets as is possible. But Ovid's *Metamorphoses* and Homer they should be very perfect in (and no other Greek or Latin) for the delight and delicacy of their fancy and the lively descriptions which they should imitate in tasks sometimes;[6] but these tasks to be in English blank verse as in Mr. John Milton's *Paradise*. But I would not have them ignorant how to make a Latin or Greek verse, and they will quickly when they master the Latin, know the way. But this exercise should be but seldom, and by the by. But for the eliciting, the inventive and the poetical faculties, and to discover and find out their geniuses, let 'em sometimes for exercises make descriptions in blank verse, or in prose; for example, of a prospect of a fair, of a fight, or wedding.

Let 'em peruse Garaei *Pia Hilaria*: there are pretty descriptions and in good Latin; the fancy not high, not much above the pitch of a schoolboy. There is a little pamphlet, three sheets in octavo, called *Artificial Versifying, a new way to make verses*, 'whereby anyone of ordinary capacity, that knows the A.B.C. and can count, though he understands not one word of Latin, or what a verse means, may be plainly taught, and in as little time as this is in reading over, how to make thousands of hexameters and pentameter verses, which shall be true Latin, true verses and good sense. Wherein the old structure of hexameters is quite taken down, and in its place a more compact one raised: to which is adjoined a new model of pentameters.' By John Peter, printed for Samuel Tidmarsh at the King's Head, at Sweetings Alley end, next house to the Royal Exchange, 1679. There is an essay of this kind at the end of Mr. Strode's *Book of Combinations*, 4to, a ridiculous hint for English metre, versifying in rhyme:

Tobacco hic		
If you be well	will make you sick.	Transposition.
Tobacco hic		
Will make you well	if you be sick	

One Dr. Webbe about the latter end of King James or the beginning of King Charles the first had an excellent way of teaching children which was printed.[7] He taught them to make verses also. Enquire for it at Mr. Crook's at the Green Dragon. There is a little book, *Pueriles Confabilatiunculae*, 1672, after Dr. Webbe's method (which get), at Mr. Crook's at the Green Dragon.

One Mr. Grantham taught boys in London to speak Latin by thirteen years of age. He printed a book about teaching children Latin sooner, which he dedicated to the parliament about 1650. My honoured friend Edmund Wyld, Esq., has it: 'tis but two sheets. He will look it out for me. He taught fourteen boys and would have no more and they learned but four hours in the day, then played, but spake Latin. Sir Edward Partridge's son, yet living, was one of his scholars. The Paul's boys were ready to knock Mr. Grantham's boys on the head. He wrote a Mastix against the schoolmasters.

The Lord Lumley speaks good Latin, taught by speaking and by a little grammar when he was a youth by Grana Portuguor, who could speak no English. Mr. Hill, a schoolmaster by the Savoy, his son learnt with my Lord, for he would learn the better to have another with him, and speaks good Latin and is a shoemaker. This I had from Mr. Hill, the father, who is an ingenious man who told me likewise that there was one Mr. Hill that did teach Latin in Whitecross Street, by speaking: he was a footman, and could neither write nor read, but learned to speak very good Latin waiting on his master at the Roman College, where afterwards they taught him to read and write. Mr. Cramer, the German amanuensis to the Royal Society, can and has taught boys of ordinary capacities in two years time to speak Latin and to understand any Latin author. When I was at Emmanuel College, there came a young fellow about eighteen or nineteen, used to come to the buttery hatch: they called him the Latin carpenter. By playing with the boys at Coventry School he learned to speak Latin fairly familiarly.

Mr. Webster, a divine, keeps a private school in Hand Alley in Holborn and teaches the Jesuit method, as Dr. Tonge did. His scholars profit by his teaching exceedingly. When they understand Latin pretty well, then they learn the second part of Alvarus's *Grammar*. Many of the priests go no further than the first part.

Mr. Roger Ascham in his *Schoolmaster* prescribes that boys should give an account of the contraries of adjectives and substantives, for example in Cooper's *Dictionary* which was in use in Eton School: according to my uncle Danvers, it opens and awakes their understanding.

Transcribe Mr. Thos. Merry's *Schema Verborum Graecorum*, in the rooms of Dr. Horneck, minister at the Savoy. It is the original and no copy, I think, has been taken of it: 'tis but one side of a sheet of paper and 'tis drawn with lines from tense to tense like a genealogy.

There is a pretty little book of four sheets entitled *Idiotismus Verbi Graeci*, Parisiis, 1636. Dr. Pell has it.

Dr. Pell told me, who taught a private school a year or two, that he taught his scholars Greek before their Latin, and that they learned their Latin easier for it. But I must find out more about this.

The Latin language is perplexed with particles and a'quivoques which make it wonderfully difficult: and these difficulties the critics, forsooth, do call elegancies. To obviate which difficulties let the boys frequently read that excellent book, Walker's *Particles*, and by degrees they will master them. But let it not be forgotten that Mr. R. Hooke, R.S.S. does much complain that all our Latin grammars hitherto are written-out grammars, and that we want a rational or natural grammar to tell us what 'love', what 'to love', *etc.* is. I do not know anyone so fit for the performance of this ingenious desideratum as himself or Dr. Lloyd, Bishop of Asaph.

While they are learning their grammar, their speech is to be formed to a distinct and clear pronunciation, as near as maybe to the Italian, especially, in the vowels; for we English, being far northerly, do not open our mouths in the cold air wide enough to grace a southern language, but are observed by all other nations to speak exceedingly close and inward, so that to master Latin with an English mouth is as ill a hearing as law-French. J. Milton [*Of Education*]

Dr. Pell would have the boys sometimes to practise the foreign pronunciation; but all pronunciations are false.

The first Latin book they should learn with their grammar should be Corderius's *Colloquia*, which are pure Latin and suited to boys' understanding. They were translated into English about fifty years since by Brinsley. Dr. Pell says it is of marvellous use. This will teach'em to construe it. Remarkable phrases should be marked with a lead-pen or red ink or the like, for them to learn by heart, and not to put them to the slavery to learn it all, which checks their spirits and keeps them back. We do not learn modern languages after that fashion. (There's since printed M. Corderius's *Colloquia*, in English and Latin, London, 1684 in 8º, by Charles Hoole.)[8]

Let them repeat the Latin Alvarus and Greek grammar every month or six weeks: only that memoriter, except in a week or fortnight some good short speech by way of *narrare* in the hall at dinner time as at Trinity College, Oxford. This task of repeating their grammar, when once learnt, 'twill be no great trouble to rehearse it.

Charles Hoole. Translation of Corderius, in columns, Latin and English, 1669. 8º.

Charles Hoole. *The Common Accidence examined and explained,* 1681, at Mercers' Chapel, 8º.

English Examples to be turned into Latin, beginning at the noun, case and verb, and after, to all the rules of grammar. For the use of young beginners at Bury School, 11th edition, London. Printed for R. Chiswell at the Rose and Crown in St. Pauls Churchyard.

English Exercises for Scholeboys, to translate into Latin, comprising all the rules of grammar, ascending gradually from the meanest to the highest capacities. By John Garretson, schoolmaster, 2nd edition, sold at the Three Legges in the Poultry, 1686/7.

Mr. Andrew Paschal, B.D., has made the *Genesis of the Real Character* with the Latin and Greek to them, which I have in MS.

Accidence commence't Grammar, by J. M., i.e. John Milton, printed by G. Symonds next door to the Golden Lyon in Aldergate. In very pretty short way, 8º.

English Examples to the Latin Syntax, by Mr. —— Walker, in Little Britain, 1683.

New English Examples to be turned into Latin, beginning with the nominative case and verbs, as 'tis varied through all the modes and tenses, and after fitted to the rules of grammar. To which are added some cautions in making Latin. Forms of the Epistles, themes, etc., sold by Brabazon Aylmer at the Three Pidgeons in Cornhill, 1688, 8º.

Dialogues by Scottenius; the most useful book for schoolboys and better by much for them than the *Colloquies* of Vives or Graevius (from Dr. Pell).

Dialogues by Chr. Helvicus; the best to begin (next after Corderius). See the first edition of this book which was printed at Gisse or Marpurg, in octavo; *ubi alternis paginis nomina et verba Textus . . . ut in Lexicis fieri solet.* Dr. Pell.

The Dialogues of Ludovicus Vives set out by Martinus Martinius, which are more useful to boys than the *Colloquies* of Erasmus (Dr. Pell).

Laurentius Valla is an excellent book.

For the French, the shortest and clearest grammar is that of M. Gabriel du Gres, where is an excellent table of verbs.

Mr. John Ray's nomenclature is more exact than that of Westminster School.

Erasmi, *Syntaxis*, or *Grammar*; also his *Verborum Copia*. *Colloquia* translated into English by —— M, 1671 at Mr. Broome's. Since that, part of it is translated by Mr. Roger L'Estrange.

John Milton's *Little Grammar*.

Ben Jonson's *Underwoods, of Public and Private Education*.

Dr. W. Holder's *Elements of Speech*, 8⁰, by E. L., a schoolmaster of Bury, used at the Charterhouse School.

Compendium Trium Linguarum, Latinae, Graecae at Hebraicae, brevi et facili methodo dispositum, by John Matterne, a Silesian (a Quaker) 1679; a pretty book.

Dr. Busby's *English Accidence*, sheets in 4ᵗᵒ, for use in the lowest forms of Westminster School.

Let the novices peruse John Ray's *Vocabulary, Latin and Greek*.

Dr. Webbe's *Terence*, grammatically Englished. Enquire in Duck Lane for Dr. Webbe's book, or books, of teaching Latin.

The Venerable Bede's *Orthography*.

Mathematics[1]

Abidas Tren, a German, has written a *Directorium Mathematicum* in Latin. 'Tis the best in print. Mr. John Collins, R.S.S., has made an augmentation of it. Both these together, he told me, will do the business. He lent it to Sir Jonas More but I could not find it amongst his papers. It is thought Mr. Flamsteed has got it but he denies it. I fear it will be stifled and lost, which would be a great pity. But Mr. Paget of Christchurch Hospital or some other ingenious young mathematician may make such another.

To add and subtract, first in small number; then to understand counters. Then to learn to write and draw and make mathematical figures. To learn and understand the axioms of Euclid: *viz. qua idem sunt = etc.* Then he will most easily learn transposition. Arithmetic thus becomes habitual: it is the foundation of justice. Alas! how heavy does the casting of accounts (so easy a thing) come to those unexercised in it—the ill-consequence whereof Mr. Osborne tells his son: but he does not tell him how he should be taught.

I would have the children learn this table of multiplication (called Pythagorus' Table) as soon as may conveniently be, *sc.* by seven or eight years old, which I would not only have them learn by rote as words, but be taught to make it themselves by addition, which is N. Mercator's way. Namely, 1 plus 1 is 2; 2 plus 1 is 3; 3 plus 1 is 4; *etc.*, up to 10. Then 2 plus 2 is 4; 4 plus 2 is 6; 6 plus 2 is 8. Then 3 plus 3 is 6; 6 plus 3 is 9; 9 plus 3 is 12. *sic deinceps*, to the completing of the table.

This method is so easy and natural that the child's tender understanding can comprehend it. An 'tis a pleasure to him to see the demonstration

1	2	3	4	5	6	7	8	9	10
2	4	6	8	10	12	14	16	18	20
3	6	9	12	15	18	21	24	27	30
4	8	12	16	20	24	28	32	36	40
5	10	15	20	25	30	35	40	45	50
6	12	18	24	30	36	42	48	54	60
7	14	21	28	35	42	49	56	63	70
8	16	24	32	40	48	56	64	72	80
9	18	27	36	45	54	63	72	81	90
10	20	30	40	50	60	70	80	90	100

of it. Whereas when he learns it merely by rote, he takes it upon trust only, and sees not the reason of it. And besides it will make a stronger impression in his tender memory. Multiplication is but a compendious addition, as division is but a compendious subtraction. And this is the first step that the child makes to get up to that wonderful, delightful and useful science of mathematics.

A child of seven years old is capable of adding and multiplying and can do as much in this as the profoundest logist. When arithmetic is not this way learnt and made habitual, it makes men almost mad, perhaps sometimes quite, that have much to do with calculating; for, not having the habit, they are apt to be out, and then infinitely running into mistakes, so confound themselves that many times they leave off. Whereas for addition, or multiplication or division we see little boys run, as it were, a gallop, and not make a false step.

Mr. Lidcot of Dublin, a learned gentleman, has a daughter of eleven years of age that understands all arithmetic and algebra, trigonometry and the use of globes, and appears at the Royal Society there. They do not find anything extraordinary in her nature to mathematics, but do impute all to her early education. (From Mr. Molineaux in a letter to Mr. [Thomas] Harley, April 21, 1686.) Doctor Holder's niece, 6 years old, going on 7, adds, subtracts, multiplies, divides and has some few definitions of geometry. Mr. Thomas Ax told me that his father taught him the table of multiplication when he was seven years of age. To write out the Greek definitions, axioms and propositions of Euclid: 'twill not only make their heads but fix it deeper in their tender memories. Besides a man understands better what he writes out than what he reads. The Greek will thus steal upon them: and so a Greek book will not scare them. Boys will add, multiply and divide as fast as a dog will trot; will run up an account like a shopkeeper. A bar-boy at an alehouse will reckon better and readier than a Master of Arts in a university or a justice of peace. Captain Charles Bertie told me that in Spain the children do learn their Paternoster and multiplication table together and rehearse it before they go to bed. The Reverend Mr. John Goad, schoolmaster of Merchant Taylors' School, has heard the same. The Earl of Pembroke told me of a French book that teaches children to number by dice. Mr. Robert Hooke says it is mentioned in the *Philosophical Transactions*. Mr. Wingate has printed a sheet called *Ludus Mathematicus*.

When the child understands addition, subtraction, multiplication and division (called algorithmus) they will quickly learn the rule of three. J. Collins would have them now fall upon plain trigonometry, wherein they will take a wonderful delight, being able with so little pains and in so little time to take heights and distances. Then let them learn the use of the globes, which they will do in three weeks' time, and next let them fall upon spherical trigonometry; and here they will be ravished with celestial pleasure.

Cuncta trigonus habet quod coelum et terram coercet.

Now, said Mr. J. Collins, it will be objected that this is a preposterous method to teach children the use of logarithms before they have the construction of them: 'tis no matter for that. They will understand that hereafter, and having espoused a love to these things they will now willingly undergo the trouble of extracting squares and cube-roots, *etc.*, which were they to learn in the first place, they would never endure the harshness of it. It would be like eating chopped hay, or taking a bitter medicine. They must be enticed only by pleasure and delight.[2]

When they understand trigonometry, let them practise it again on

Gunter's sector and quadrant, which is of quick use and dispatch; and understanding the use of globes they will perfectly understand the use of Stoffler's astrolabe, of the use whereof is lately printed a pretty treatise, a stich't 4°, by ——. Sir Geoffrey Chaucer wrote a treatise for the use of the astrolabe for the use of his son, which is amongst his works. He begins thus: 'Little Lowis, my sonne, I perceive well by certain evidences thine abilitie to learne sciences, touching numbers and proportions, and also well consider I thy busy prayer in especiall to learne the treatise of the astrolabie. This treatise will I shew thee in wonder light rules and naked words in English, for Latine ne canst thou not yet but small, my little sonne.' It seems by this introduction he was but ten years of age. When they do understand the use of globes and the doctrine of spherical triangles, they will be able to run a gallop in astrology. Then let 'em make use of their arithmetic in reducing the planets' places. Most of them will take a wonderful delight in it. It would be a great use if it were only an allurement to make 'em in love with mathematics, but surely there is good use to be made of it, and it is capable of much improvement. Leovitii *Astrologia* is a clear method; so is Argol's and H. Coley's *Astrologia*.

Seek of Dr. Pell what is the best idea for children to have of numbers, and as to addition and subtraction, in mind. For example, $7 + 5 = 12$, add the 2, which see, as it were, in your imagination. The vulgar do it, I suppose, by the remembrance only of the sounds of the names of numbers. Or is it better to make their idea by the imagination of the pips in cards? This for children of seven or eight years of age. But together with their algorithmus I would have them learn literal algebra, which is very easy for them. When they are perfect in their algorithmus and have gone through their trigonometries, I think that they should be informed in the first six books of Euclid's *Elements*, and when they are masters of the first book, they will easily learn and understand surveying, in which they will take a great pleasure. But this belongs to the next chapter. About the beginning of Queen Elizabeth's reign— Hill [Hylles] printed the rules of common arithmetic in English verse. Sir Ch[arles] Scarborough has it (which see).

Let the copies which they write be mnemonic verses of arithmetic; for example, Mr. Nath. Sympson's, or those in the roll-pressed arithmetic book in 4° by ——. Mr. Street's mnemonic verses in Mr. Seller's *Navigation*, also Dr. Edward Davenant's for algebra. So they will have a double learning by a single task. But Dr. Pell does not at all approve of this way. He would have 'em remember the way of working, as he does, which makes a stronger impression in their minds and is more useful.[3]

My honoured friend, Anth. Ettrick, Esq., has told me that he got ten thousand pounds by his knowledge in computation of estates. For example, (*inter alia*), a copyhold of twenty pounds *per annum* at 14 years purchase in 25 years pays principal and interest at £5. per cent. Buy the last edition of Philip's *Purchaser's Pattern*; and see Sir Jonas More's and ask Dr. J. Pell concerning these. Find out Mr. Edmund Wyld's way of proving division, after the cancelled way, by adding the division below and the remainder above and equate the dividend. This way he learned of old Mr. Speidell. Mr. R. Hooke has invented an excellent way of division, which I must get. Mr. Nich. Mercator says that the best way of proving addition is to add it up backwards: the casting away of nines is sometimes fallacious.[4] The teachers of merchants accounts in London make them cut off the uppermost and lowermost sums and then cast up and add them.

Desire Dr. Pell to print his *Tariffa* for the ease of working division, which he says is useful both to learners and the learned.

Let them cast up (to exercise their skill) the account of the house—£200 or £300 per annum—and see and learn the method of household examples which they may use themselves to good purpose when they are housekeepers.[5]

Let them have Dr. Pell's table of 10,000 square numbers. He advises me that the mathematical boys should make his tables, which will make their heads, as also to make the table of incomposits for division. Above all things, let 'em be well instructed in that admirable and great rule of algebra, by which a man may be *mathematicus αὐτάρκης*, and having but pen and paper may, without help of books, satisfy his own desire in solving of questions.

'From algebra, all sciences mathematical have their foundation. Therefore the first and immediate part to be learned being attained to with less time and difficulty than either arithmetic or geometry, hitherto delivered. Also, the author is ready to make it appear that no person unacquainted with algebra shall ever come to that perfection in arithmetic and geometry as in six months time a child of ten or twelve years of age shall attain to. More-over, a scholar, in a month's time by this method in algebra shall know more in arithmetic or geometry than otherwise he could ever have comprehended.' [John Ward's *Advertisement*.]

Let 'em learn to cast accounts with counters after the French fashion (and in Queen Elizabeth's time, used in England). In the library of the Royal Society is an old book, *sc.* Jo. Martini, *Silicaei Arithmetica*, in folio, Parisiis, 1519, in practica et theorica scissa: ubi elaborate agitur de computatione per calculos (I think), to astronomical fractions. Alstead (I think), says that it is the quickest way of extracting roots, difficultly learned by books, but easily learned by an informator. Sir Chrst. Wren says that algebra might be applied to counters and improved.

Let 'em every day after supper solve a question in algebra to make it become habitual to them to keep up their arithmetical faculty. When they solve problems let them ever use that excellent method invented by Dr. John Pell, by steps, in the which is like a Jacob's ladder that reached to heaven—a way of working in perfect syllogisms from the beginning to the ending. 'Tis like Jupiter's golden chain, described by Homer. After Dr. Pell's way of solving questions a man may take a nap and fall to work again afresh where he left off, which one cannot do according to the Oughtredian method. The like method may be used for solving cases in the civil law. A Polish gentleman, Libinitius, a Socinian, complimenting the Doctor in a letter which I have seen calls it *divina illa margo.* (He was cut to pieces by the papists in the highway.)

Aristotle in his *Ethics* doth declare, were orders of justice
limited and by the degrees of the estates in the commonwealth
established, and although that particular may be called geometrical,
yet it will appertain to the art of arithmetic. O in how miserable
case is that realm when the interpreters of the law are destitute of
good sciences, which be the keys of the laws. How can they
either make good laws or maintain them, that lack true knowledge
whereby to judge them. Dr. Record.

In the solution of problems, Mr. N. Mercator's way is to reduce things *ad minima, qd. N.B.*

Let them exercise their wits (to make them ready) in considering the square tiles in chimneys and marble pavements—from the Reverend William Holder, D.D., sub-dean of his majesty's chapel. Begin at an angle and account all the progress sideways till you come to the opposite angle: 1, 2, 3, 4, 5,; 4, 3, 2, 1, which added together make 25, the square of 5. The greatest number this way being what is found but once; all the rest twice. 1, 2, 3; 2, 1—3 by 3, namely 9. 1, 2, 3, 4; 3, 2, 1—16. All the use the Doctor made of it was to propose a seeming difficult question which was really very easy. But the question of as high as 15 or 20; the naming of 20 numbers to be added seems a long work, but taking only the square 1, 2, 3, 4, 5; 4, 3, 2, 1 added 25, of the greatest number amongst them is soon and easily done.

5	4	3	2	1
4	5	4	3	2
3	4	5	4	3
2	3	4	5	4
1	2	3	4	5

Let them peruse Dacheti *Mathematica Ludicra*; Sir. Willm. Petty's *Duplicate Proportions*; his *Observations on the Bills of Mortality*; his *Politic Arithmetic*, written for King Charles II (Sir Joseph Williamson has it), *etc.*, to exercise their logistic faculty. Let 'em peruse Sir Jonas More's *Duodecimal Arithmetic* in his *Vade Mecum*, for, and at the instance of, Sir Robert Long, Auditor Auditorum; and desire Sir James Long, his nephew, to look for it amongst his papers, for there it is more fully expressed than in the aforesaid book.

Transcribe the method of household and stable accounts that the Right Honourable Nicholas, Earl of Thanet, used, which was that of the Duke of Tremouille in France, which is very good but very operose. I gave it to Sir John Hoskins, Knight and Baronet. Consider the fallacies that may be imposed by bailiffs in their accounts or by the ill posting of them, which James Collins observed in great men's accounts, and told me how 'twas, which I have quite forgot; and since, he is dead. Mr. —— Osborne in his advice to his son, tells him that he has known many men of good estates, have been undone merely for the want of skill in a little plain and common arithmetic. I have known young persons of great quality at the Academy in Paris that at eighteen years old know not how to cast up pounds and shillings and pence as they ought. Sir Edward Leech was wont to say that carelessness was equivalent to all the wasting vices.[6] A banker in Lombard Street, Rob. Welstead, assured me to his knowledge, that most tradesmen are ruined for want of skill in arithmetic; for merchants sell to them wholesale and the retailers, through ignorance, overshoot themselves and do not make their money again.[7]

Let 'em learn anatocism which [teaches] them to understand simple and compound interest, annuities, values of leases for lives, and for years; *sc.* so much rent, then the fine what? Let such a debt lie so many years; see what it will amount unto. A hundred pounds *per annum* rent, then what must the fine be, for so many years or so many lives?

Last of all, let 'em learn merchants' accounts, to keep an account technically: as also for the better managing of their own estates. And it will teach 'em method, that ten thousand things shall not confound them. When they are perfect in arithmetic, they will be masters of it in three weeks time.[8] This art of accounts is a very good qualification for a master in Chancery. Otherwise, they never understand cause, but through ignorance they haze and perplex the cause more—which most commonly they do—and then leave it after a great deal of money spent to be decided by the merchants. In Holland and in Hamburg they have court merchants to determine such matters, which is the best way. Wherefore, Anthony, Earl of Shaftesbury, intended, had he continued Lord Chancellor, to have their causes before trial, first clearly and exactly stated by Mr. J. Collins, R.S.S., which would have been worth to him £800 per annum.

The Prince of Orange employed Symon Stevins of Bruge to bring in better order the tactics, which he did, which is now the modern way of military discipline. The Prince, seeing that so much was to do with the knowledge of mathematics, put him then on methodising accounts, which he also did. So, had it not been for the Prince of Orange, S. Stevins had not been what he was; and had it not been for S. Stevins, the Prince of Orange had not been what he was; of such use were they to each other.

Ask Sir William Petty how many years lives do live, one with another. What is the medium of all lives; whether fifty or sixty years, and his *Observations on the Bills of Mortality, de hoc.* Ask also Mr. Thomas Ax for his demonstrations that a lease of three lives is better than the landlord's reversion in fee; which also Anthony Ettrick, Esq., positively and knowingly affirms. Ask Mr. Ax for his calculations of Sir William Portman's Old Rents; namely, that they do yield but two pounds per cent except in the aguish moors of Somersetshire (which note).

Concerning the proportion of purchases, now money is at £6 per cent, is but sixteen years purchase and a quarter. Michael Davy has

writ of this subject, and so has Mr. Samuel Moreland. See Mr. ——
Philip's *Purchaser's Pattern*, and find which the best edition of it.
*A President for Purchasers, Sellers and Mortgagers, or Anatocisme and
Compound Interest Made Easy*, by W. Leybourn at the Black Swan
in Holborn. (See if it is considerable.)

The proportion of raising taxes in a country: for example, Thomas
Flud of Kent, Esq., a worthy and learned gentleman. See his rule for it.

Dr. Pell says that the main thing in algebra is the right stating of the
question; for when the question is well stated it will evoke itself and
the like is to be said for law cases. Cicero in his *Orator* says that a good
understanding client comes to him and puts his case clearly, and he
understands it. The lawyers come to plead it before the judges and
confound it, and the judges do not understand it. Dr. Pell says that for
the solution of questions there is required prudence and a natural
mother wit, as well as a knowledge of the axioms, but use and practice
will much help nature.

He told me that one Jeremiah Grinken, a mathematical instrument
maker, frequented Mr. Gunter's lectures at Gresham College. He
used an instrument called a mathematical jewel by which he did speedily
perform all operations in arithmetic without writing any figures, by
little sectors of brass, or some semi-circles, that he did turn, every one
of them, upon a centre. The Doctor has the book, now amongst the
rest of his papers in the custody of Dr. Busby: he told me he thought
his name was Prat. It is in 4to.[9]

Let them have Sir Samuel Moreland's solids cut in wood to understand postulates the better: they are curiously engraved.

Plato says, take away arithmetic with measure and weights, from
all the other arts and the rest that remaineth is but base and of
no commendation. Where, although Plato do name three things
in appearances—number, measure and weight, what are measure
and weight but numbers applied to several uses, for measure is
but the numbering of parts of length, breadth and depth. And
so weight, as here it is taken, is the numbering of the heaviness
of anything. So that if numbers were withdrawn, no man could
either measure or weigh any quantity. And therefore it must
follow that number only makes all arts perfect. . . . Without
it all arts are but base, without commendation. This may
suffice for the just commendation of arithmetic But yet one
commodity more which all men that study that art do feel, I

cannot omit. That is the filing, sharpening and quickening of the wits that by practice of arithmetic does ensue. It teaches men so certainly to remember things past. So circumspectly to consider things present, and so providently to foresee things that follow that it may truly be called the file of wit. Yea, it may aptly be named the schoolhouse of reason. The like judgement had Plato of it, as appears in his words in the seventh book *de Republica* when he says thus: 'They that be apt of nature to arithmetic be ready and quick to attain all kinds of learning. And they that be dull witted and yet be instructed and exercised in it, though they get nothing else, yet this shall they all obtain, that they shall be more sharp witted than they were before.' What a benefit that any thing is to have the wit whetted and sharpened. Dr. Recorde in the Preface to *Whetstone of Wit*.

My ignorance and want of a good, early mathematical education has made me write this idea more feelingly (perhaps) than a more learned man would have done.[10]

Sir William Petty's Duplicate Proportions; done by my learned friend Mr Nicholas Mercator

Theorem I As the root of the number of cannons to the root of another number of cannons of the same size and strength, so is the distance at which the first number of cannons is heard to the distance at which the second number of cannons is heard.

Cannons	Root	Distance at which the cannons are heard
1024	32	160 miles
4000	63	315 miles

Theorem II As the root of the length of one pendulum to the root of the length of another, so is the time of the first pendulum to the time of the second: and inversed. As the square of the time of one pendulum to the square of the time of another pendulum, so is the length of the first to the length of the second.

Time	Square	Length in inches
1st 1sec.	1	32 inches for one second of time
2nd ¼sec.	½	8 inches for half a second of time

Theorem III Of the proportion of the weights of the powder and the distances of the shot and the time of flight. The weights of powder are the squares of the distances, or the distances are as the roots of the weight.

1st Example. The weights let be four pounds of powder, and one pound. I demand the proportions of the distances.

As the roots of 4, that is 2, to the root of 1, that is 1; so is the distance which the bullet flieth that is fired by 4 pound to the distance of another bullet that is carried by 1 pound.

2nd Example. Let the proportions of the distances that the bullets fly be treble, or a 3 to 1; then to find the weights of the powder, say:

As the square of the lesser distance, that is the square of 1 being 1, to the square of the greater distance, that is the square of 3 being 9; so is the lesser distance to the greater distance.

Theorem IV As the roots of the distances which the bullets fly, so the time which they are in their way; or inversed. As the squares of the times which the bullets are in their way, so are the distances which they fly.

1st Example. Let one bullet fly 100 yards, and another 49, which is near half the first. I demand the proportion of the times they are in their way.

As the root of the greater distance, that is 100 being 10, to the root of the lesser distance, that is 49 being 7; so is the time of the first bullet—admit 20—to the time of the second but 14.

Theorem V The proportion of the weights being given, to find the proportion of time. As the squares of the times, so are the proportions of the weights.

Example. Let the time be as 7 to 10.

The square of 7 is 49 and the square of 49 is 2,401. The square of 10 is 100, and the square of 100 is 10,000. So is the weight of 1 pound to the weight of 4 pounds very near.

Dublin, 29 May, 1678

Mr. Aubrey,

As for the opinion of Dr. Woods and others, that the emanations of visibles, audibles, *etc.* should have been in triplicate proportion, not duplicate proportion, I say that neither is demonstratively true, but that duplicate doth better agree both with reason and experience.

Carpenters and wheelwrights say that the diameter is to the circle as 1 to 3; others say better, as 7 to 22, but neither is exact yet both serve the turn. So what I have done in that discourse was only to keep men from gross errors and for bringing them into the way of exacter truth. I hope no man takes what I have said about the moun[t] and burthen of horses and the living and dying of men for mathematical demonstrations. Yet, I say, they are better ways of estimating these matters than I had ever heard from others. I hope better are now found out. But there are two or three real mistakes in that treatise which more *per* next.

I am,
Yours, etc.,
William Petty

13

Geometry*

Let them be taught the first six books of Euclid and let the demonstrations be those of Bellinger's [presumably Billingsley] *Euclid* or those of the Greek *Euclid*, which Dr. Wallis says are as good as any, or better; but set down after Dr. Pell's way. Let them always have Barrow's *Euclid* in their pockets. They will in half a year's time get through these six books, and that with delight, and infect one another with their knowledge. Let 'em draw the schemes themselves, which will make a fast impression in their fancies that they will see it, as it were, by the strength of imagination in the dark, and in their beds.[1] And let them write out the demonstration of any proposition which will make them apprehend it the sooner and remember it the better. As they go on in their demonstrations, and do perfectly understand the proposition, and readily demonstrate it, let them read the same proposition in Greek and learn the text by heart. Thus, Greek will insensibly steal upon them, knowing before the sense, and thus they will be led on to understand Ptolomey's *Almagest*[2] in Greek and then they will be tempted to read Polybius or other Greek authors. Let them have perfectly, by heart, all the definitions and axioms in Greek.

I would have them understand the second book of Euclid's *Elements* by those clear demonstrations of Dr. John Pell which are done on one side of a sheet of paper most curiously, fifty years since. They are in Dr. Busby's hands. I thought to have transcribed them but was surprised by his death.

Let them gradually with their learning be taught the use of instruments; for example, the theodelite, plain-tables, cross-staff, sector and

* See also Appendix A.

circumferentor, for the measuring of land. And after some practice let 'em make guesses of acres, heights, distances (*praeter propter*); namely, such a ground is so many acres; that is about twice that bigness, thrice, *etc.* In Livy, [they] guessed at the height of a wall of a city by numbering the squared stones or bricks. This habit may be of use in many cases, *sc.* to know 'tis no bigger, or more than.[3]

Let 'em practise to measure timber. For the practical way see —— by —— of Sherborne in Dorsetshire, 16 ——, in 4to sticht, a useful book; and Mr. Browne's two sheets. Note, in the circles of trees cut horizontal and see what difference in diameter between six years growth and eighteen years growth: that as to coppice wood. Let them understand the best way of felling timber. (Ask if to fell, top, lop and bark be the best way. E[dmund] W[yld] Esq. says 'tis.)

> It happens to many to discover by signs and sometimes by their actions, their resolutions which the tongue hath kept silent. It is also necessary for a commander to understand the mathematics and the theories, especially of astrology and geometry, the art whereof is not very necessary in this trade, yet the use may help much in the alteration of things. The chief necessity consists in the consideration of the day and night. If they had been always equal there would have been no difficulty therein. Polybius, *Histories*, *lib.* IX.

Occasion is the mistress of all human affairs, but especially in the art of war. See where Homer commends Ulysses for his skill in astronomy for land and war as well as navigation.

The use of geometry for taking of heights and distances for scaling walls:

> wherefore it is necessary for them that will aim truly in their resolution of the course of war to know the use of geometry, if not perfectly, at least that they have the knowledge of proportion and consideration of similitudes as also for the comprehension of designs in the situation of a campaign. Therein for the tactics, of which he wrote commentaries. Not only many people, but even commanders and captains are amazed and wonder how it can be possible that the city of Lacedaemon (48 furlongs) should be greater than that of Megalopolis (50 furlongs) seeing the circuit is less; yet it is twice as great as that of Megalopolis. And consequently they conjecture the numbers of men by the circuit of the camp. Polybius, *ibid.*

Dr. Record's *Whetstone of Wit* in the preface, says,[4] Plato thinketh no man able to be a good captain except he be skilled in the art of arithmetic and we account it no part of those qualities that be required in any such man. Howbeit, for the trial thereof, I have in this book formed some of the questions in such form as they may approve the use of this art, not only good for the captains but most necessary for them, so that without it, they cannot marshal their battle, view their enemy's camp or fort. And if I shall say as I think, without it a captain is no captain.

Let them be taught mechanics which is comprised very clearly and ingeniously in two sheets in French (a manuscript) of the five mechanical powers. It is of great use. Of all studies there is not any so useful to mankind as this is: and all the rest of mathematics are but in order for this. Let those who have a good natural genius this way, practise to vary the operations; for example in the sixth chapter of Oughtred's *Clavis*, namely, *alterne*, composite, division, converse, for begetting and improving invention. This will be of very good use and will discover fine and useful things.

Old Herbert Westphaling, Esq., had a very mechanical head, but not much geometry. After you came within his gate you saw a great variety of mechanics—almost every lock and bolt different from the vulgar.

As a supplement to Sir William Petty's excellent *Advice of Mechanics*, I would have boys that are mechanically given, to learn the tin-man's trade which will be greatly useful for making of models: 'tis easily learned and two or three tools will serve their turn.

The Greeks did maintain public professors, whom they called *tactici* to teach their youth the practice and art of all forms convenient for military service. One Mr. Alexander of Colen, that Sir Joseph Williamson brought into England, has reduced this art clearly and succinctly into two or three sheets of paper at the most and taught it in London, with other mathematical sciences. (Get a copy of it of Captain Wynd in Drury Lane, over against Drury House; and —— of the Tower has all his original manuscripts.)

Valour alone will not advance a soldier to a command without art. He may have the favour to play at trictrac in the general's ante-chamber, but never to be elected one of the council or have an office or be made a man of conduct.

Let them be instructed in the rules of perspective, which is very easy and let those whose *genii* do incline them to it, by intervals and for their recreation, practise drawing. I would have these lovers make perspectives of walls, of cyprus trees and of pillars, in level, uphill and downhill, which is easy to do, there being no difficulty of draught in it, and extremely pleasant to the eye. This will train them to draw figures in perspective, which few painters understand. It will prepare and fit them for starting in landscapes, and indeed for the drawing of everything that is drawn from life. Then let them practise to draw horses as big as the life on sheets of paper pasted together. This will make them to understand horses better than other men. Let them draw a greyhound standing: it is reducible to a square and oblong. Sitting, it is to be reduced to Pythagorus's rectangled triangle, *sc.* three, four, five. And to teach 'em from the master lines of the circle, square or triangle, not to be confounded [by the] multiplicity and variety of lines, but by finishing the draught by off-sets, as in surveying, for example.[5]

Let 'em practise to draw circles, ovals, squares, oblongs by hand, without the help of compasses or ruler. Also let them draw the penman's flourishes and knots, which will wonderfully make their hands for portraiture. Captain Richard Bertie, methought said well that as the bones of the skeleton are the foundation of the muscles so is a square or oblong the foundation of drawing. He makes all his faces, breasts, hands, arms to grow from squares. Now by this graphical exercise, I do not intend or expect to have them Titians or Van Dykes, but I would have them to proceed so far as to be able to draw prospects of engines and to express their own inventions of them. By this education also, though they do not attain to great mastership, yet they will be able to judge of drawing rightly.[6]

Digby, Bishop of Limerick in Ireland, divertised himself with limning and does it very well, but that is too effeminate. Painting is more masculine and useful. See Mr. Sherwin's *Drawing Book*: he promises there another method of circles, squares, etc., for drawing.

Let them portray the little twopenny maps of the world—black'd paper placed under the map or picture and another paper between, and then trace it over with a bodkin. 'Twill leave the exact impression on the underpaper. Then draw it over with ink. This will fix the idea of the planisphere in their memories, then, if they will, let them do the like by a sheet map, or the like; or a hemisphere projected from a pole, and afterwards when they are good proficients let them make the same projection with their compasses, *sed in regulas Ptolomei.*

His Highness, Prince Rupert, was an excellent draughtsman: he drew with his own hands the draught of the sections of the ships, and sea-fights which Mr. Wenceslaus Hollar has etched, and Mr. Thompson sells them. James Long, Esq., was in that memorable action with Admiral Herbert at Bugy,[7] where he showed much courage and conduct, and which action he drew and engraved, to our satisfaction and use. A prentice of a surgeon who took a delight in drawing, drew over the draughts of an anatomical book, whereby it is so fixed in his memory that it is of much advantage to him.

Statics, music, fencing, architecture and bits of bridges are all reducible to the laws of geometry. Nay, ——— Gunning, Bishop of Ely, proved by geometry that there was a deity, which demonstration Mr. Smythwick of Westminster has.

Let 'em understand dialling for the natural way, first by the globes and afterwards by the sector.[8] Let 'em practise to take heights and distances by the cross-staff. Let 'em, when understanding, be informed in the astronomy of Mr. N. Mercator. By this time they will be able to understand Ptolemy in Greek. Those that continue in this school till seventeen or eighteen may be instructed in the conics: and let them have a cone cut and divided neatly in wood. And they may be able to peruse Archimedes.

But now let me return to Euclid again, which is certainly the best book that ever was writ.[9] We have several good Euclids but we still want, as Dr. J. Collins said, an algebraical Euclid. Dr. Barrow's is only a symbolical one. He said, 'Agree but upon the definition of proportion, and the rule of three will be demonstrated, and then you may demonstrate the triangle.' He did give me a pretty instance of the definition, which was by ——— of a logarithm, which I have forgot. Ask Mr. Paget of Christchurch Hospital *de hoc*: I believe he does remember.

A good, substantial yeoman would think his money and his son's time ill-spent when after seven years study he should tell his father he had found an equation between a sphere and a cylinder. [Sir Walter Raleigh's name is inserted in the margin here.] To which I [Aubrey] would add that he would take it for a resverie [reverie] to hear him affirm that the knowledge of solutions of curious questions in arithmetic and geometry should qualify him for the study of understanding of the laws and case-divinity, but it is certainly so, which Vieta and Firmat, both justices, well knew.

It is the best way of teaching to reason; makes them tread sure steps and keeps them from concluding hastily. When I was a schoolboy at Blandford, there was at the Bowling Green a gentleman, a German, that was driven out of his estate and country by the wars that raged there. He was forced to maintain himself by surveying land. He told the gentleman that it was good to have a little learning; no one knew to what straits or shifts he might be brought. 'Before the wars,' he said, 'I had as good an estate as any of you'; which expression I took much notice of. Had this gentleman been bred only to understand genus and species, he might have wanted bread; and besides his want of mathematics, he would not have had the address, or been conversable, *è contra*. The Right Honourable Edward, Earl of Hertford, was wont to say that if he were to earn his living, he had no way but that of the fiddler, and thus were several great persons bred in those days. Music is a great thief of time and if one love it never so well and has a genius for it, a common fiddler, or barber, or footman must needs outdo him; they making it their continual practice. The late King of Spain [Philip IV] spent the greatest part of his time in playing on the tenor-viol: as for matters of estate he left that to be managed by ——, his minister of Estate. It argued a most magnanimous soul in the present Louis, King of France, of whom the Archbishop of Paris in the life of Henry IV says of him, being then but a youth, that he had rather have no crown than not to govern himself. He (his majesty of France) cannot play on the fiddle, but he can make little towns great cities and make devastations of great cities and countries. He understands perfectly fortifications, the besiegings and making approaches to cities or castles which he was taught when young, not only by linear draughts but by works raised in earth. And he has in his cabinet at the Louvre very curious models of fortifications in cabinet work. It ought not to be forgotten that his majesty, King Charles II, though a prince of peace, did understand fortifications as well as any man. He had a mathematical genius, but wanted early education. He was wont to divertise himself at Windsor with such military draughts and designs and did invent a new —— in fortification unknown before. Mr. N. Mercator has proved ingeniously to me that his majesty understands fortifications as well as he did.

Sir Jonas More was wont to say that the ancients did certainly understand algebra; for else they could never have found out those propositions handed down to us: but they concealed their trick. My country friend, old Mr. Tho. Flud of —— in Kent, told me that Malapertius has writ on the six books of Euclid, but on the fifth book he is the best of all others.

My impatience and eagerness when I read Euclid, without a teacher, to run on too fast without digestion; *ergo*, better for a boy to be read to lesson by lesson. I would have them carry in their coat pockets Barrow's *Euclid*, but no farther than the ninth or tenth book, not only for lightness of carriage but to avoid their being perplexed by running on too eagerly.

Some wits, moderate enough by nature, be many times moved by overmuch study and use of some sciences, music, arithmetic and geometry. As these sciences do sharpen men's wits overmuch, so they do change men's manners oversure, if they be not moderately mingled and wisely applied to some good use of life. Those that be wholly bent to the mathematics, how solitary they be; how unfit to live with others and how un-apt to serve in the world. This is not only known by common experience, but uttered long since by wise men's judgement and sentence. Galen saieth much music marreth men's manners, and Plato saieth the like in his *Republic*, translated by Tully.   Roger Ascham in *The Schoolmaster*.

The rules of prosody do teach boys to make verses, but it is their mother wit (genius) that makes 'em poets. So Mr. Harriot's, Mr. Oughtred's, or Dr. Pell's rules teach them algebra, but they must have a good mother wit and logic too, to become inventors and promoters of mathematical learning.

14

Ethics

Next, I would have their understanding opened with the ethics, but not by Cicero's *Offices* (as the common fashion at schools is); though it be an admirable book, 'tis unfit for boys. Dr. Ralph Bathurst tells me that Pufendorf's *de Justitia et Jure* begins with ethics admirably well. The ethics we read at Trinity College, Oxford, are well-digested, clear and short, compressed in six books (they say by John Prideaux, D.D., Regius Professor of Theology), which they will quickly get by heart. Now they will know what virtue, what vice, justice and its opposite, injustice, have the characters of the passions. From hence I would have them to read Mr. Hobbes' *Human Nature* which is the best; P. Charron's *de la Sagesse*; Monsieur Senhault's *of the Passions*; Lord Bacon's *Essays* and M. Montaigne's. These will furnish them with matter enough for their *chrias*. Then, having tasted of this moral knowledge, let 'em read Aristotle's *Ethics* in Greek, to improve their Greek together with the science, but skipping over the tedious discourse of the *summum bonum*.

But above all, let 'em perfectly understand *justitia universalis*, and *particularis*, being the foundation of religion, law and politics; and it is the very basis of ethics. Cicero, in the first book of *de Natura Deorum* says 'religion is our justice and gratitude toward God.' Lord Herbert of Cherbury says, '*honor est conscientia moralis*'. But this is natural justice in whose minds it dwells and is derived from the stars, so that every one is not an idoneous bearer of ethics; indeed, but very few; namely those who have sweet, even and harmonical souls given them from God. Our Saviour's sermon on the mount is, as it were, the quintessence of all, distilled in an alembic.

I remember a saying of James Harrington, Esq., several years ago,

that if we endeavour to go an inch above virtue, we do fall an ell
below it. This as to the enthusiasts and fanatics. Unequal tempers
are biassed with some particular passion, *ergo*, unjust; *ergo*, not fit
auditors of morals; not apt to imbibe it; *ergo*, not fit to be judges,
magistrates. I reflect on that text in *Luke* 9: 55, 'ye know not what
manner of spirit ye are of.'

In Homer are excellent descriptions of the passions, in so much that
Horace prefers him to be read before Chrysippus and Crantor (in
lib. 1, *Epist.* 2). When passion is stronger than reason, then men act
according to the dictate of their passions, which commonly they do.
They know well enough they do not according to reason. The greatest
rogue in Newgate knows as well that he commits a sin as the greatest
divine. So 'tis clear that men do act according to their passions and not
according to their interests. If a man did act according to his interest, a
politician could better foretell what he would do than a good astrologer. As Mr. Hobbes says, as often as reason is against a man, so often
is a man against reason. The greatest sinner knows that he commits a
sin as well as the greatest casuist.

> Atque nefas tandem incipiunt sentire peractis
> Criminibus tamen ad mores natura recurrit
> Damnatos fixa et mutari nescia.   Juvenal. *Sat.* 13.

Let 'em make observations themselves of *mores hominum*. It may be
said that that is as old as Homer, but the application of it to youths
(for the making it become habitual to them so early) is as well now as
useful. Wherefore, I would have 'em read mankind daily, as well as
books, and to insert their observations *in adversariis* in a pocket note
book.

A young gentleman, a friend and kinsman, going to travel, waited
on the wise William [presumably, Robert], first Earl of Salisbury, and
desired his advice. Said his Lordship, 'All the advice that I give you is
this, that every man that you meet, believe him to be the greatest
knave in nature, but do not tell him so, for then he will be angry with
you.'* It is not to be imagined by a sweet-natured young person that
has been virtuously bred, what rugged, dogged, churlish natures some
people have. 'With the froward thou shalt learn frowardness' *Proverbs*
[in fact, *Psalms*, XVIII, 26]. But it is the greatest providence and goodness of God to give us caution of such bad people from their counten-

---

* See p. 133

ances and aspects. *Foenum habet in cornu.* Horace [*Sat. lib.* i, iv and xxxiv].

Let 'em imbibe, if possibly, Dr. Pell's assertion that one can never attain to perfection in mathematics, or any other science, that does not profess truth above all things. Let there be drawn up for them a catalogue of moral and useful questions. Let there be severe admonition against scoffing and mocking. 'For it is He that hath made us and not we ourselves' (*Psalm* 100, v. 2).

I would have the aforesaid college notes put into the Real Character.

Jhesus Sirac says, 'neither to thy foe ne to thy friend discover not thy secret, ne thy folly; for they will yeve you audience and looking and supportation in your presence, and scorn you in your absence. Scarcely shall you find any person that can keep a councell secretly. Whilst thou keepest thy counsaile in thy heart, thou keepest it in prison: and when thou bewrayest thy counsaile to any wight he holdeth thee in his snare.' 'With scorners he make no company, but fly her words as venome,' Sir G. Chaucer [in the *Tale of Melibeus*, Sec. 20 and 31].

Sir Thomas Pope's motto, *Quod tacitum velis nemini dixeris* [Attributed to St Martin, Archbishop of Braga, *c.* A.D. 560].

Comedies are good to open youths' understandings as to *mores hominum*, to what we call humours, namely the delirations from morality and prudence. After they have learned *memoriter* the epitome of the ethics (before said), it will please to read T. Randall's comedy called *The Muses' Looking Glasses*, which is the ethics put into a play. This will but define them and make a deeper impression. Then at spare time they may divertise themselves with Shakespeare and Ben Jonson's comedies. Green's *Tuquoque* is a useful play, though not for the tooth of critics. (See Horace, *lib.* i, *Sat.* 14; *lib.* i, *Epist.* 2).

Logic*

When they have gone through Aristotle's *Ethics* in Greek, then I would have 'em go over Euclid again with the demonstrations of Dasipodius which are done in syllogisms, which will train them to be logicians and know how to make a plain syllogism.[1] And I warrant by this time they are proficient in the six books of Euclid. Thus the boys first learn to sing plainsong before they learn descant. Now let them read Dr. Sanderson's *Logic*. But I would have 'em begin with the second and third book first, *sc.* propositions and syllogisms. Then let 'em read the first part, which is metaphysical and which is like *The Seaman's Dictionary* to the *Art of Navigation*. Of all the parts of logic, the fallacies are the least written of, and the least studied and practised, but the most use. And the detection or untying them is an excellent exercise for young men's wits. They are all to be reduced to the ignoration of the elenct,[2] so that the understanding of the Real Character will much help them and be a great furtherance to this work.

Being now furnished with matter out of the *Ethics*, let 'em practise to dispute on easy and useful questions and let their informator teach 'em to draw consequences and how to impose or untie a fallacy, of which let there be provided and made for them a good penus. Dr. Sanderson says in his *Logic* that no exercise does improve young men's wits so much as disputation.

Tomitanus, an Italian, has expressed every fallacy in Aristotle, with divers examples out of Plato, the best that I have seen, though a Jesuit might have done it better. Mr. Ascham says that Cambridge did commit this fault, *sc.* in reading the precepts of Aristotle without

* See also Appendix B.

the examples of other authors; but Mr. Smith, Mr. Cheke, *etc.*, did put to their helping hand.

The logic notes of Trinity College, Oxford, are as good perhaps as any are (by Bishop Prideaux). They are short and clear: we learned them by heart. In teaching it is the best and most delightful way for youth first to see a prospect (as from a mountain) of what the science is, and then they will be the better encouraged to take a long journey thither. Also, it is good for them at last to close with a compendium.

I do not know of any little treatise that has so much logic and close reasoning in it as *Felo de se* writ by Mr. Tomb against Mr. Baxter, a stitcht quarto scarce so big as an accidence. I do not recommend this as to the verity and propagation of his doctrine which is Anabaptism, but for the keenness of it, being writ, not *oscitanter*, but with a good deal of spirit and animosity. Their parties sometimes would fight, a matter of 200 of a side. One lived at Kidderminster; the other at Beudley.

I have heard some young sophister say that Burgherdicius's *Logic*, with the notes of —— is more clear than Dr. Sanderson's, but I much doubt it. Joachimus Jungius, Hamburgenensis, *de Demonstratione*, not yet printed, is the best treatise of that kind, Dr. Pell tells me, that ever was writ.[3] He did print a logic before, but he said that that was *Logica Hamburgensis*, but this he kept as a secret. He was, Dr. Pell says, a good mathematician; which made him demonstrate so well. Mr. Theodore Haak tells me since that he thinks it is printed since his death. Inquire for Mr. Jo. Milton's *Logic* which I think is not yet printed.

Mr. —— Tomb, B.D. was wont to say that to be a good logician, 'tis requisite that one should also be a good grammarian. To define well is the main thing, wherein is need of the grammarian's skill: the Real Character will be also of great help for this; besides there is another material requisite which is to state the question rightly and clearly. But this is more of mother wit, God's gift, than art.

Let 'em make themselves masters of topics. Let 'em peruse Peter Heortado[?] ——, Summulists,[4] who treat of the particles namely, *tantum, solum, etc.*, inclusively negative; for which reason they bring one out of the way, and fallacies are often imposed upon one.[5]

Let 'em peruse Castanei *Distinctiones* which, perhaps, they may use symbolically. But Mr. Hobbes was wont to say that distinctions are but cobbling. Let men define well, and there will be no need of distinctions.

Let 'em peruse some mean writer to the end to find out his paralogisms, to confute him: and thus, by degrees, they will learn to confute
more able writers.

I shall end this chapter with a saying of Sir William Petty's who
observes that the great logicians out of the schools are the least persuasive men in the world. The reason is plain; they want practical and
prudential mediums. So they bring that excellent art into disgrace.
Not that the fault is in the arts, but for want of a *Penus Rhetorica,
Politica, Oeconomica, Ethica* and for want of conversation amongst
men and business.

My learned and worthy friend, Mr. Thomas Fludd of Kent, Esq.,
informs me that Dasipodius has written upon all Euclid ('tis an old
book) but his way of writing is by syllogisms and that 'tis the best
way in the world, he says, to teach logic. I, discoursing of this matter
with Dr. Chr. Wren (since Kt.), he tells me that Euclid's *Elements* are
not fit for logic: but is the reverse of it: 'tis enthymeme; and if you
begin at the bottom and go up, 'tis syllogism. Let this be considered.
Let 'em peruse *The Logician's Schoolmaster: or a Comment upon
Ramus, his Logic,* by Mr. Alexander Richardson, sometime of Queen's
College in Cambridge, London, 1629.⁶

Rhetoric

As to the figures in rhetoric, I would have them learnt by the by, as it were: *sc.* with the same pains and the same time that they learn to write, and their copies should be the figure-rules in verse, either Latin or English, as shall be thought fittest.

In Mr. Johnson's *Advice* are rules enough to train on a child to this art. When they are perfect in it (suppose 16 or 17), let 'em read Mr. Hobbes' *Rhetoric*, which is Aristotle's, in English, excellently modelised by him, and short. And then to close, let 'em read it in the original Greek. Bishop Sanderson said that he had read over Aristotle's *Rhetoric* not less than sixty times. Let 'em always remember to *collineare*.

The advice of the reverend father Drexilius in his *Aurifodina* to a preacher is to make his sermon a syllogism. The like rule is to be observed in their *chrias* and declamations. There are certain declamations of Quintilian, lately translated into English—they say well— [to be had] at the west end of St. Paul's churchyard.[1] The heights and sweets of M. Balzac's laboured pieces are incomparably smooth and courtly. See also the *Apology* of M. Balzac. The rhetorication of the preachers generally is not close enough: too lax and vague, like Pindaric poetry.

I presume and require that by this time they perfectly understand all the passions. Let a subject be given them to declaim, or rhetoricate upon, which has been worked on by some great master of eloquence— *The Roman* of Balzac, or the like—and let them do their best and then compare their essay with the other to see how short they fall of the other's excellency. Then let 'em take the topics of the author, cut like valentines,[2] and try to come as near as they can to the master's method and disposition of them; also for the wording. Then compose both again, and so, by degrees, as in learning to write or draw by imitating a good copy, at last, by assiduous endeavour are come to equal it and to do as well as the original.

Let 'em peruse those excellent orations in T. Livius, a table whereof by way of division as to several members, fitted for all sorts of speaking or writing, and digested according to the several places of the three principal heads of all causes in oratory, namely the deliberative, the demonstrative and the judicial, at the end of Philemon Holland's translation.

Horace says in *lib.* I, *Epist.* 19; *O imitatoris servum pecus* as to style, and Milton:

> —— a preposterous exaction used in most of our schools and universities, forcing the empty wits of children to compose themes, verses and orations, which are the acts of inept judgement and the final work of a head filled by long reading and observing with elegant maxims and copious invention. These are not matters to be wrung from poor striplings like blood out of the nose, or the plucking of untimely fruit: besides the ill-habit which they get of wretched barbarizing against the Latin and Greek idiom with their untutored Anglicisms, odious to be read, yet not to be avoided without a well-continued and judicious conversing among pure authors digested, which they scarce taste; whereas, if after some preparatory grounds of speech by their certain forms, got into memory, they were led to the praxis thereof in some short book lesson'd thoroughly to them, they might then forthwith proceed to learn the substance of good things, and the arts in due order, which would bring the whole language quickly into their power. [*Of Education*][3]

I would have them sometimes for a variety of exercises make extemporary declamations or themes. 'Tis good exercise for young men to declaim, for it will make them good orators. The theme being given them, after a quarter of an hour's premeditation to furnishing themselves with topics, to word it extemporary, *sur le champ*. The use of this will do them great service hereafter in common discourse, narrations, *etc.*, and when they shall have occasion to speak on the sudden in either the House of Lords or Commons. I have heard some ascribe the great readiness and well-speaking of the French to their children's reading so much of romances. Dr. J. Owen did acknowledge this, and so has Mr. W. Penn of Pennsylvania, to me.

Instructions concerning the Art of Oratory, printed at Oxford, 1682, exemplifies most of his ornamental topics by instances drawn from Pliny's *Panegyric*. Pliny husbands each particular circumstance to the most complete advantage, and gently strains most of his occasional hints beyond their natural tendence, which though an un-comely exercise in familiar narration is a confessed embelishment to a more free discourse.   Preface to the translation of *Pliny's Panegyric*, by White Kennett.

Let 'em be shown how to draw out and improve hints which is the life of invention, as the birds teach their young to fly first by fluttering from sprig to sprig. John, the Earl of Rochester, improved his sister, Mrs. Whatton's natural wit by showing her how to improve a hint in poetry, and 'twas his Lordship's familiar and frequent way in discourse to take some very ordinary and trivial subject and never let it alone, never leave twisting, till he had made wit of it. So I would have the informator of the oratory to show them how to improve their hints in oratory. First let the scholar do as well as he can; then let the master show him how to draw it out, yet further: *sc.* give 'em two or three periods or paragraphs, as plain song, and show them how to descant upon it and draw it into branches. So lute masters play along with their scholars. By this way, when once they have got the knack of it, provided they have ingenious souls, their wits become luxuriant as a vine, and will run away with it at a main rate.[4]

Civil Law

After they are perfect in the Ethics, let 'em be introduced in the principles of civil law,[1] in order to do which let them read thoroughly, and digest, that excellent book Johanis Jacobi Wisenbachii *Disputationes ad Instituta Imp.*, a 4to, 1676, which is the best author for a beginner that I ever met with, or have heard of. And as they read it, or are rather read unto by the civil law informator, let 'em, as before in the Ethics, be taught how to draw consequences, and that *more algebraico*, and to detect paralogisms or fallacies.

Cicero's *Offices* may be read. Let 'em read next *Paraphrase des Institutions de l'Empereur Justinian*, par M. Pelisson, a thin 8°, 1664 (excellent). Read Suarez *de Legibus* which Isaac Barrow, D.D., said was writ as demonstrative as Euclid or Archimedes, as you may see expressed in his life before his sermons, writ by Mr. Abr. Hill, R.S.S. Read St. Thomas Aquinatis *Secunda Secundae*, so much commended by Bishop Sanderson who told Seth Ward, Lord Bishop of Sarum, that he had read it no less than sixty times over.

The civil law is the mother of the common law, and heretofore, *sc.* in the time of Henry I, the common lawyers of this nation mixed their studies. Note, for Fabian Philipps says our common lawyers nowadays—nay the judges themselves—are ignorant both of the civil laws and feudal law. And as for the records of the Tower, they never foul their fingers, but lap out of Sir Edward Coke's basin. Sir Orlando Bridgeman, Lord Keeper, advised young students to begin with the civil law.

Mr. John Selden, in a manuscript of his, 4to, which the Earl of Abingdon has, speaking there of the civil and common laws, said that the reports alone teach not a man law. Mr. J. Selden was a good civilian, so was Mr. Matthew Hale: and Sir John Maynard is pretty well acquainted with it. When they leave this school they may then study the *Institutions* of Justinian with the commentary of Monsignor Vinnius.

Let them read Geo. Feltmannus, *de Feudis*, a little book in 12mo and then let their informator read to them the first book of Littleton's *Tenures* and how these tenures came: *sc*. 'tis feudal law; but neither Littleton nor Sir Edw. Coke tells us so. Suppose a young gentleman goes from hence to the Inns of Court, he will be able thus armed to *natare sine cortice* and not stand in need of assistance of anyone there to help him in his studies. The common lawyers would have young men kept in ignorance, and so would the peasants as to husbandry.

Judge Doderidge was an able lawyer and they say a good man: he wrote a book, a thin 4to, entitled *The Lawyers' Light*, wherein he lays down his law arguments in syllogisms.

When they enter upon the study of the common law, let them peruse the *Commonwealth of England*, writ by Sir Tho. Smith, who has declared summarily, as in a chart or map, the form and government of England. 'Tis best to read Littleton's *Tenures* first several times without Coke's *Comments*, for, for a novice to begin to jade his patience, 'tis as one that begins geometry with Clavius upon Euclid.

A compendium drawn out of Mr. Sharrock's book of about the bigness of a Cato would be very useful to initiate youths in ethics and civil law. Great books are at first too tedious to children, and by an abridgement they may be drawn on with delight. Mr. Merret of the Inner Temple, has reduced the common law to a method by Dr. Wilkin's way (the Real Character) which was believed before to be impossible. The Lord Chief Justice Hale, hearing of it, desired to see it and he was satisfied with it.

At the Inns of Court the young gentlemen read Littleton's *Tenures* with Sir Edw. Coke's *Commentary*. When the commentary came out, they expected to have found the reasons of the law, and he gave us his commonplace book, for he made Littleton his topics. But Mr. Polyxfen's advice of the Inner Temple, is to read over Littleton's *Tenures* first without a commentary. Rob. Stephens, Esq., of the Inner Temple, Sergeant at Law, my worthy friend, was wont to say that a young student of the common law ought first to read over and thoroughly *Naturae Brevium* to make himself master of that book, and afterwards he would easily understand the common-law books.[2]

Let 'em examine Sir Edw. Coke's *Reports* according to the method of des Cartes. I doubt not but that there would be discovered several paralogisms. As well as these are, I do believe, five hundred false translations of the Latin and French statutes, in which languages they were originally writ. As to the reports, the judges are most commonly old men and by the time they have got home and dined, they have forgot much of their reports, so that we have them imperfect. And as for the records of the Tower there recited, Sir Edw. Coke trusted to his clerk to transcribe 'em, which Mr. Francis Duffield, M.T., and William Swayne, M.T., have had the curiosity to compare with the originals, and there are, I'm sure, several places materially erroneous.

Young students in the law are advised to keep company with those that are better lawyers than themselves, else the worse lawyer gets of him, and he reaps no benefit by the conversation of the other.

At the Inns of Court they do not learn the rules of justice *ab origine*, but instead chicanery and *trickum legis*, the art of wrangling and illaquention, overreaching and oppression. They do learn the law after such a manner, as if to solve questions in the mathematics. One should resort to Bettinus's *Apiarium* and *Ærarium*, and do things *per fac simile*. Whereas an artist works analytically, as, for example, in Mr. Peyton Chester's *Exercitations*. I remember a grave barrister of the Middle Temple and a good student: he had a great memory and would have quoted any case in the reports, but had you put a case to him, altering but the very name, he was at a loss and a stand, could go no further; just like a greyhound when the hare is mashed through the hedge, he could not hunt it out. And for the Synderisis,[3] they have generally sense only of equity when they lie on their death beds. Erasmus says they are *omnium doctores in doctissimum genus*.

The common lawyers have been the men that have obstructed the Bill for Registers; for example, at Taunton Deane, where they live so free from law-suits and can take up money to the last acre of land.[4] Gentlemen thus bred would be able to bear up against them in Parliament House and take up the cudgels.

Tully in his book, *de Oratore*, says that when a client comes and tells his case, he understands him, but many times it happens that when his lawyer pleads his cause, he does it so perplexedly that the judges do not understand it. This is as to the well-stating of a question, which being well done, the question will almost work itself.

Let them apply their analytical learning to the solution of *Juris Universalis Problemata* after the manner of Renatus des Cartes in his

Treatise of Method. There is in High Dutch an historical proceeding of a law-suit, from the beginning to the ending—very pretty and useful.

The result of this education is that young gentlemen will be qualified for the House of Lords and Commons, for ambassadors, and referees in their country amongst their neighbours.

When the young gentlemen have, suppose by eighteen, finished this cursus, to what place should these pretty, tender plants be removed? To our universities? They would learn but little there: the university scholars would rather learn of them. But they would be in great danger to be debauch'd by their idleness and luxury. I should rather be of the opinion to send them to Leyden where they would not only improve in the civil law, but in their speaking of Latin and French; besides, they would get a little Low Dutch which is no contemptable language. There are excellent books of mathematics and chemistry in Dutch.

Mr. Thomas Hobbes says, were it not for the laws, that many men would not make so much a scruple to kill a man as I or others would to kill a little bird. Sir Edward Leech would always put off his hat to the gallows: he gave God thanks he lived under a government, for were it not for the laws—*homo homini lupus.*

Mr. Miles, scrivener, did understand merchants' accounts, which did him great service: he also studied grammar, as to English, for avoiding amphibologies and pinchings in conveyances, but the Real Character is yet much better for this purpose or intention.

Mr. Thomas Hobbes says in his *Leviathan* that men will never be obedient and good subjects till his doctrine be taught in the schools.[5]

18

Politics and Economics

Let 'em peruse Aristotle's *Politics* and peruse Dr. John Case's *Politics*; and also, after that, peruse Sir William Petty's *Political Arithmetic* (it is not printed), and his *Political Arithmetic of Ireland,* which is printed, 8º.

Let 'em understand the several methods of settling government after conquests; for example, of the easterns, by transporting of the conquered; of the captivity of Babylon, which way they still use in those eastern parts. Of the Romans by garrisons; of the Goths by the conquest and by holding by knight service, whence came our feudal levies. Methinks the Gothic method is the best of all.

See *Idea Œconomicae et Politicae Doctrinae* by Franco Burgherdicius, *opus posthum.* Lugd. Batavorii, 1644. 'Tis a pretty enchiridion in 12º and fit for them to begin withall; of which, when they have given a full account, let 'em read Aristotle's *Economics* and *Politics* in Greek, and so let the Greek tongue steal upon them.

Economics

Read Aristotle's *Economics*: it is short and clear. The illustrious Cecille, Countess of Oxford, married afterwards to the Earl of Elgin, made an agreement with the cook for the kitchen stuff wherefore the most nourishing juice of the meat will be lost, thorough the cook's covetousness.

A whore is a most pernicious thing in a family and will infect the servants like a plague. T.M., Esq. [Thomas Mariet, of Whitchurch in Warwickshire?]

The economy and methods of accounts of such a society as this is will sufficiently inform them hereafter for the government of their own families.

19

Mundane Prudence

As concerning mundane prudence, although it may be true what Ovid says in *Metamorphoses* (*lib.* VI) *seris venit usus ab annis*; yet this generous education will accelerate it.[1] Let 'em have good books to read as Mr. Osborne's *Advice to His Son*, the Earl of Shaftesbury's *Advice to His Son*, Sir Walter Raleigh's *Advice to His Son*, Charron's *de la Sagesse*, Norden's *Dialogues*, Montaigne's and Bacon's *Essays*, and then after the manner prescribed here, repeat after a little recollecting. The distiches of Cato and the quadrans of Pibrac are good when their stomachs are ripe for them, but pedants give them moral precepts too early, namely at ten or eleven. The study of the law makes 'em prudent as to the understanding of their estates, as to title, *meum* and *tuum*.

Good books are as a means of faithful advisors, they flatter not, they discover those things in law, husbandry, *etc.* which those that possess it would conceal from them and keep as a mystery. *Felix quam faciunt aliena pericula cautam* (Juvenal). It is this that makes old people more wary and jealous and so prudent than young people, because they have seen more experience. (Not but that the reasoning of young people is as good as the old, and their apprehensions quicker.)

My uncle, Judge Jenkins, commanded his son to say every morning as soon as he was awake, this verse from Horace (*Epist.* I, 18):

Quid de quoque viro et cui dicas saepe caveto.

This, he said, may be a means to preserve your life, by preventing you from engaging in a quarrel. And the advice of Achilles' father to him (Homer's *Iliad*, *lib.* IX, by Mr. Thomas Hobbes):'

My son, said he, when you take leave from Troy,
May Juno and Athena strengthen you,
But this one lesson take from me I pray,
Remember still your anger to subdue,
Decline all contestation with the tongue
And let your conversation gentle be.

Courtesy, or common civility is the cheapest thing in the world and the most useful. Great men do understand well the respect that is due unto them, but they also know what is due from them to their inferiors. Aristotle makes contempt the ground of all discontent, there being never anything taken offensively but *sub ratione contemptua*, and least wisely apprehended. Solomon in sundry places interprets all acts expressing a mocking or despising our neighbours not without a strong reflexion upon God himself, as tending to the contempt and dishonour of their Maker. (Bishop Sanderson's *Sermons*, vol. I, Sermon 3.)

Admit thy brother, shallow in understanding and judgement, or deformed in body, yet the community of nature and humanity should be sufficient to free him from contempt, his body framed of the same dust, his soul breathed by the same God, and he is thy neighbour. (*ibid.*, vol. II, 1.)

Above all things to avoid magisteriality because it creates envy: it draws on affronts and scorn. When a man enters upon the stage of this wicked world he must deny himself, even as the Adepti* do; he must scorn ignorance, he must become all things to all men. But let him be careful to avoid the conversation of scorners, for he can get nothing by them but envy and contempt. Note Sir Geoffrey Chaucer's character of a young knight—

That from the time he first began
To riden out, he loved chivalrie,
Trouth, honour, freedome and courtesie.

Let them read at times, for example in rustication, *The Rules of Civility*, translated out of the French into English, an 8°, about half an hour at a time, no more. *Human Prudence*, by which a man may raise himself and his fortune to grandeur, by A.B., 3rd edition at the Angel in Cornhill, 1686, and *The Work of a Penny* by H. Peacham, M.A., 1677.

Sir Wadham Windham, one of the judges of the King's Bench, his

* I.e. those who possess the secret of alchemy.

advice to his son, Colonel John Windham, was: 'Set down all your expense, and then', said he, 'spend your estate if you can.' 'This advice,' said the Colonel to me, 'has done me almost as much good as the estate he left me.'

> Spare not, nor spend too much; be this thy fare,
> Spare, but to spend, and only spend to spare.
> Who spends too much may want, and so complain,
> But he spends best that spares to spend again.

I have read this distich somewhere:

> Thy credit wary keep; 'tis quickly gone,
> Being got by many actions, lost by one.

Suppose one should lay an injunction on a young man to remember this saying of Polybius, *Avaritia est morbus in favorabiliter*, it would be of good use to him when he is engaged in worldly commerce; for then, when he shall deal with an avaricious person, he will do it with all the caution and circumspection he can.

Take general acquittance from traders once a year for a little honesty goes a great way with them: they make no conscience of telling a lie, and most of them are knaves.

A young gentleman that was going to travel came to my Lord Burghley to take his leave of him and desired his Lordship's advice how he should carry himself. My Lord replied that every man you meet and greet are great knaves, but you must not tell 'em so, for if you do they will be angry with you.* Polybius says, 'No beast so savage as man', of which things the beginning and greatest part do proceed from the lewd life and breeding of youth. John, Earl of Rochester, says ingeniously somewhere, that for a man to be honest is as if one should play upon the square among rooks.

'Most men, but that they speak and wear fine clothes, as to their understanding and morals are beasts.' (Juvenal.) Nay, I once saw sparks of justice and detestation of oppression in a brave, brinded-mastiff dog in Jermyn Street, that for the sake of righting wrong fell severely on a great, cruel mastiff that was worrying, and had near killed at the windpipe, a poor, little, harmless cur.

The observations of physiognomy will be of great use to them, of which let every one keep a *Penus Physiognomica* by him. It is an infallible rule to discover you the indications of pride, treachery,

* Aubrey also attributes the story to the first Earl of Salisbury. See p. 117.

passions, *etc.*; and, having this, to avoid their conversation and obviate their wicked designs.[2]

'Watch and remember, that thou most distrust' was a saying of Epicharmus quoted in Polybius (*lib.* xvii).

The way of dealing with this wicked world is a kind of tricker-trick and wit (and why not here?) to take advantage of plots, *etc.*, to be quicksighted for that. Knaves take a wonderful pleasure in why-nots and oversights, not at all regarding commutative justice, or what Cicero says is done *bona fide*.

When a man's genius does strongly impel him to do, or not to do, a thing, obey, or follow that divine impulse. See also Dr. Henry More concerning this. Mr. John Needlar of Gray's Inn, a very discreet person, has protested to me that he never did succeed in any business when he went against his own impulse, although he had very persuasive reasons from prudent friends.

Not to cohabit with one who has a genius ascendent over him, for it will fret his soul out of his body and kill him. For example, let no servant be so for his son's sake, unless he has a mind to have his son's spirit broken and his wit spoiled.[3]

I cannot forget the advice of —— Matravers, a poor, distracted man (for discontent) of my neighbourhood, but he had good, lucid intervals; namely, whosoever does purposely make you drunk is not inwardly your friend. Mr. Andrew Marvell's rule was not to drink liberally to inebriation with anyone with whom he would not entrust his life. 'Too much drink makes quarrels arise.' 'Tis an ale-house song, but true.

> —— ad summum bonum, propositum totius vitae tuae, respice.
> Illi enim consentire debet, quicquid agimus; non disponet
> singula, nisi cui iam vitae suae summa proposita est. Ideo
> peccamus, quia de partibus vitae omnes deliberamus, de tota
> nemo deliberat.   Seneca, *Epist.* LXII.

20

Foreign Travel

The cursus of this school being now finished, I would in the next place have them travel beyond the sea, unless they would go through a cursus of chemistry. The martialists may go from hence to a campaign. Travel does much open the understanding, and besides gives a good address. I have heard an old friend, Fabian Philipps, say that Queen Elizabeth did cut out so many ingenious young gentlemen out of the universities to send to travel *pro bono publico* in order to make them ministers of state. This the learned Society of Jesus knew right well, who send their company from one college to another. No doubt but there are some men of as good natural parts in other colleges, but being acquainted one with another seven years or more, to converse with them is like thinking oneself; besides it makes them speak Latin well. Mr. Lassalls has writ the best directions for European travels. His opinion is 'tis the best way to begin with Holland and Germany, or Switzerland and return by Italy and France, for he says the frippery of France, especially at Paris, would too much allure them to vanity and make them disrelish their more serious and useful studies. Let them stay in Germany so long that they understand a Dutch author. For chemistry and mix't mathematics no language does afford so many good books. No nation is so much addicted to chemistry in so much that the very country people do understand distilation and can make extracts, especially in Tryol and Miesen, and above all Gosler in Low Saxony. (This good note I had from my honoured friend, Mr. D [ethlevus] Cluverus, R.S.S.)

Let them in their travels observe husbandry and economy and all ingenious and useful engines; of architecture of rooms of use, as kitchens, barns and stables, cow-houses and pigsties; and in these things Holland does most excel. They are now entered into the dangerous time of temptation of love, which by staying at home they would infallibly fall into—lawful or unlawful—but being kept in action, body and mind, in a strange country they will not be at leisure to be attacked by Cupid.

When they return home, I would have them travel several parts of England where they may make curious remarks. Scarce any country has greater variety of natural things. When they are twenty-one years of age, or on their return home, let 'em read John Norden's *Dialogues*, *sc.* between the lord of a manor and the steward, between the lord of a manor and his bailiff and between the lord of a manor and his surveyor.

Instructions for rent gatherers. Accounts made easy, by the author [Stephen Monteage] of a book called *Debitor and Creditor*, London, at the printing press in Cornhill, 1683.

Some fathers do send their sons abroad to travel and they do well in it, but few do take care to train them up to understand their estates, as if afraid to let them be acquainted with that mystery, the want of which proves often of very bad consequence. They ought to be well-informed in the buying and selling of timber. The Lord Lovelace's father, who aggrandised the estate, advised Sir Robert Henley's father to make his purchases in a woodland country. I have heard a friend of mine, say, who had great woods, that selling timber by the foot was not the best way. 'Tis better, he said, to sell by the lump; *sc.* top, lop and bark—to every 50 feet of timber, ten shillings for top, lop and bark. The heaving and carriage is pretty considerable. (*Sed quare de hoc.*)

21

Epilogue: or the conclusion

The education of children has been by several writers thought fit to be the care of public magistrates, and so such a design as this. No man goeth about a more godly purpose, than he that is mindful of his own and other men's children. The end is to render young gentlemen such as are elegantly described by the satirist in these verses:

Esto bonus miles, tutor bonus, arbiter idem.   Juvenal, *Sat.* VIII.

Gratum est quod patriae civem populoque dedisti,
Si facis, ut patriae sit idoneus, utilis agris,
Utilis et bellorum, et pacis rebus agendis.   Juvenal, *Sat.* XIV.

These qualifications this institution will give: but how little that of the universities contributes, the effect shows. The tutors in my time, were generally ignorant in arithmetic and geometry. They read to them logic, then exercised them to dispute on dry logical questions which nauseate the young gentlemen and make them loath it. They teach 'em to make syllogisms and to dispute before they are furnished with the mediums—'ergo Potlid', says Charron. And so, instead of giving to young gentlemen the accomplishment according to Juvenal, they return home with learning (if any at all), of a Benedictine monk, with some scholastic canting. Thus, in lieu of giving him the breeding of a gentleman, he is sent home with that of a deacon. Now, as when a man has false buttons on his doublet, he must be fain to unbutton all again to set it to right, so those:

quibus arte benigna,
Et melior luto finxit praecordia Titan.   Juvenal, *Sat.* XIV.

137

after they have left the university, do unlearn all again and begin anew.

This institution will teach 'em to be *fabri sub Fortuna*. That noble and ingenious knight, Sir William Petty, my honoured friend, from a small stock of riches did gain by his surveying in Ireland, several thousand pounds per annum, honestly and ingeniously. In like manner, Mr. [Richard] Foley of Staffordshire, who had a little common arithmetic, and being led by curiosity to see the slitting mills in Spain, has left an estate of £5,000 per annum. Knowledge is a sort of riches, whereof there can be no deception; they cannot be pillaged. It will make them live in peace and war.

By this education, when they are eighteen or nineteen years old, their genius will appear, to what it is inclined. Boys have as many, or more, maggots (as they call 'em) in their heads, than men. Now this way of education will find work for them and matter enough for 'em to bite and feed on—drawing, mechanics, chemistry, perspective and the rest.

God almighty is the giver of gifts: to excel in any art or invention is God's gift. We have it from our genitures and from the stars. Sir Anthony Van Dyke or Sir Peter Lely could not teach his desciples to be equal to himself. So in mechanics, of all gifts the most useful to mankind, oratory, poetry, *etc.* 'Tis true, those that are dull, or of ordinary understanding, may obtain to some degree of skill for their way of living, calling or station; as every man cannot attain to the skill of dancing on a rope, but, as my Lord Bacon says, he may learn to walk on the rope.

All have not parts to be scholars, but those to whom nature has not given to be such, will like this institution well, that they will breed up their sons after this way, and recommend children of their friends to be thus informed. A dunce may have a prodigious wit in his son, and *vice versa*, as we many times see. Sir William Petty told me when he was a boy, he did understand all trades in Rumsey, his native place, a màrket town in Hampshire—namely, watchmakers, smiths, dyers, and the rest. Now as to this institution, I think it would be very fit to have them see chemical operations, as, suppose, the physician of the college at his laboratory, to become acquainted with that curious, spagyrical art, and so to become in love with it, which will be a useful and ingenious diversion and excitement to them; namely, to make their own medicines, especially if they live in the country. And this they will learn in one month.

Now the gentlemen thus instituted are qualified for lawyers, ambassadors, commanders by land or sea, architects, solicitors, chemists and surveyors. Astrology is the best guide, to direct us as to what professions or callings children are by nature most fit or most inclined to.

My friend Sir Edward Harley, Knight of the Bath, was wont to say that he had rather trust his estate to an ingenious education than to a sheepskin (meaning a deed of entail). It will make 'em disrelish and contemn base and ignorant conversation.

The good, natural parts of youth, for want of due and timely education, are rusted and, as it were, grown over with moss, by rustic conversation, and their wits drowned withall like tosts, to their own loss and their country's. Precious stones unpolished are but pebbles; so wits uncultivated are but of vulgar understanding. As there are stones of different worth, which by polishing are become all glorious (though not all diamonds and rubies) even so amongst youths, by education. They all gain a lustre, but of a different degree, according as the giver of all good gifts has been pleased of his grace to bestow them.

By this institution they will be as knowing at eighteen as generally men are at thirty-six; a great difference of time, and a great gain.

Mr. Abraham Cowley and some others have designed colleges for a generous education, which require ample endowments. Here, in this *Idea* is only set down a method, very plain and practicable, and here is required only the bringing together of so many (suppose five or six) able informators to be sent for from abroad, which is no difficult matter, and providing a convenient house for them.

H. Plattes in his *Superficial Treasures* says 'that he that can find out an improvement in husbandry, doeth more good to the common-wealth than he that founds fifty almshouses.' (For example, Mr. Firmin, who maintained —— hundred weavers, spinners, *etc*.) In like manner, whosoever could procure such a way of education, would do more good to his country than if he had built and endowed several colleges in the universities.

Now though the expense of this education be as great, or perhaps greater than that of the Inns of Court, yet there will be compensation for it hereafter, for when they are admitted to the Inns of Court, or when they travel, the expense of their fine learning, for example in mathematics and dancing, will be superseded, as being perfectly learnt and understood already, and much better than it would be then and there in a more adult age. They will have nought else to do at the Inns of Court but to study the municipal laws, nor in their travels but to learn the languages, see things worthy of remark and make observations.

It is a great pleasure to behold a fine plantation of cypresses or cedar trees; but *a multo fortiore* a greater to see the flourishing of young plants, to see how they thrive and what shoots they make in their learning. *Quantum lenta solent inter viburna cypressi.* Virgil.

Methinks it is a great pleasure to me to consider and foresee how many young gentlemen's minds would be cultivated and improved and their understandings opened by good information of sciences, as the sweet rose-buds are opened by the morning dew. How much would learning receive an advancement in this way, and how many patrons and Maecenases would spring up to encourage learning and learned men. Whereas, on the contrary hitherto, seed has been sown on a rock, which has generally either withered or degenerated into wild oats, unless by God's wonderful providence, five or six in an age come to be eminent in mathematics. And but few are economical to their country, or themselves and their concerns.

But now, methinks, I see a black squadron marching from Oxford, set up by a crozier staff to discomfit this pretty little flock. And so this pleasing dream is at an end.

Soli Deo Gloria

Appendix A

[To illustrate the practical value of mathematics, Aubrey includes in his *Idea* the following essay by Samuel Foley. 'I believe,' he comments, 'that Sir William Petty had a finger herein.' Petty, perhaps the most attractive of the *virtuosi*, a dynamic, cultured and exceptionally versatile man, had shown in his economic studies how statistics of the kind which were later to be used in actuarial calculations could be applied to the problems of land valuation, population, and life expectancy. In a similar vein is Foley's attempt to bring the logical method of the geometrician to bear on the business of managing an income prudently in order to extract from it at various periods the greatest satisfaction and utility.]

Mr. S. Foley's letter to the Royal Society touching the application of mathematics to the ordinary concourse we have in the world.

To the Royal Society at London,

Gentlemen,

I have made trial how some few thoughts relating to the common concourse of mankind would look in geometrical dress, and take the boldness to present them to your honourable Society. I know your readiness to encourage all endeavours after useful knowledge; therefore presume you will show some little favour to this attempt of mine, it may be, so far as to recommend it as a hint to others of a more happy genius to prosecute either this argument, or some noble subject, upon such sort of principles as these. I have no excuse to make for the meanness of my performance, but that I know not that this was ever aimed at by any man till now.

Your most humble servant,

Dublin, 1685

Computatio Universalis sive Logica Rerum

Being an essay attempting in a geometrical method to demonstrate an universal standard whereby one may judge the true value of everything in the world.

Advertisement

The design of the following essay is to put people in a right method of good husbandry, and to assist them to procure as much happiness as is procurable by them, by showing them how to compute their time and riches, and to compare them with other things.

Definitions

1st Definition
By time, or the age of man, I desire may be understood all that part of man's life which he can employ after such a manner as he himself judgeth convenient, and therefore after he has come to the use of his reason.

2nd Definition
By a man's estate, I understand all the wealth and riches of which in the time of his reason he is master, and has at his own disposal, whether it be by the kindness of his relations or as the fruits of his own industry.

3rd Definition
By happiness I understand all the care and satisfactions and pleasures a man can procure by his estate, and which do not come upon him without his own choice and forecast.

4th Definition
By wisdom, I understand a skill and a resolution to procure all happiness that can be procured by such a man.

5th Definition
By a fool, I understand one who either does not know how or does not resolve to procure all happiness that can be procured by him.

6th Definition
By pleasures, I understand all sorts of innocent diversions, conversations, plays, gaming, hunting, hawking and the like, according to men's different fancies and inclinations.

Postulata

1 That in order to the making of a better comparison between things it may be allowed us to fix upon a determinate number of years, and to call that the apparent age or time of a man.

2 That upon the same account, it may be allowed us to fix upon a determinate sum of money and to call that a man's apparent estate.

3 That it may be allowed us to subduct from the apparent time and from the apparent estate of a man, all those parts of his age and wealth which are not at his own disposal.

4 That the value of time may be expressed by a proportional value in money.

5 That it may be allowed us to assign different pleasures and satisfactions to the different stages and periods of a man's life. And till a more probable and particular and exact one be offered, to make use of the scheme following, namely:

	From	
1st period	9–16	All school learning, such as grammar, writing, arithmetic.
2nd period	16–25	All sorts of trades or academical learning, travel and pleasures and exercise suitable to that period.
3rd period	25–36	Recreations, courtships, pleasures suitable.
4th period	36–49	Honours, preferments and pleasures suitable.
5th period	49–64	Increasing of riches, of power and interest and pleasures suitable.

Axioms

1 Time is as necessary to enjoy happiness as an estate is to procure it.

2 The same proportion, that the whole happiness of a man's life bears to his whole real time and true estate, the same proportion do the distinct parts of happiness bear to proportionable parts of his real time and estate.

3 Happiness is worth as much time, and as much money as are absolutely necessary to procure and enjoy it.

Propositions

1st Proposition
If a man do live from his birth to the end of 64 years, that is 64 apparent years of time, his real time or age is but 32 years.

Demonstration By the first definition, such a man's real time is only that part of his life which he can employ as he himself judgeth convenient after he is come to the use of his reason. And therefore, by the 3rd postulate I make the following subductions:

	Years	*Months*	*Days*	*Hours*
1 For childhood, before he begins to use his reason to good purpose	9			
2 For sleep, because he cannot employ that time in the purchase and enjoyment of satisfactions as he pleaseth, at the rate of 8 hours in 24	18	4		
3 For devotion, reckoning that as God's time	3	6		
4 For sickness, such as disables him from taking satisfaction in the things of the world, at least	1	2		
The sum	32			

The sum of the subduction being 32 years taken out of the apparent 64 years, the remainder thereof, which is the man's real time is 32 years.

Which was to be demonstrated.

2nd Proposition

If such a man has an estate of inheritance of £120 per annum, his whole real estate is £4,940 sterling.

Demonstration   By the second definition, his true real estate is only so much of his wealth as in the time of his reason he has at his own disposal, and therefore by the third postulate, I make the following subductions.

The whole sum arising from the £120 per annum during the 64 years, without interest or any other improvement amounts to £7,680. Subducted out of it:

1 For the nine years of his childhood		£1,080
2 For charity, being God's and the poors' money, and public taxes, being the magistrates' and his country's money, a tenth		£ 660
3 For clothes, necessary		£ 420
4 For food, lodging, just necessary		£ 480
5 For unavoidable expenses in sickness		£ 100
The whole sum of the deduction		£2,740
Therefore the remainder is		£4,940

Which is the real estate: *quod erat demonstrandum.*

3rd Proposition

The whole happiness of such a man's life is worth 32 years and £4,940.

Demonstration   By the 3rd definition, the whole happiness of a man's life is all the ease and pleasures and satisfactions which he can procure by his estate during the whole of his life time. But by the first proposition, the time of such a man's life is 32 years, and by the second proposition his estate is £4,940 and by the third axiom, happiness is worth as much time and as much money as are absolutely necessary to procure and enjoy it.

Therefore the whole happiness of such a man's life is worth 32 years and £4,940. *Q.E.D.*

4th Proposition
Such a man is wise if he does know how, and resolves to procure as much happiness as is worth 32 years and £4,940.

Demonstration By the 4th definition, wisdom is skill and resolution to procure all happiness which man can procure. But by the 3rd proposition, all the happiness of such a man's life is worth 32 years and £4,940.

Therefore, such a man is wise, if he knows how, and resolves to procure as much happiness as is worth 32 years and £4,940. *Q.E.D.*

5th Proposition
Such a man is a fool who does not know, and resolves to procure as much happiness as is worth 32 years and £4,940.

Demonstration By the 5th definition, that man is a fool who does not know how, and resolves to procure all the happiness which can procure by him. But by the 3rd proposition, all happiness procurable by such a man is worth 32 years and £4,940.

Therefore, such a man is a fool if he does not know and resolve to procure as much happiness as is worth 32 years and £4,940. *Q.E.D.*

Corollary Hence it follows that such a man is a fool if he lays out upon a particular and determinate part of the happiness of his whole life more than 32 years and £4,940 than that particular part of his happiness has proportion to his whole happiness. For by the 2nd axiom, the same proportion that the whole happiness of a man's life does bear to his whole time and estate, the same proportion do the different parts of his happiness bear to proportionable parts of his time and estate. Since, therefore, he is a fool if he does not know and resolve to procure as much happiness as is worth 32 years and £4,940, he must be a fool if he gives more than 32 years and £4,940 for any particular part of his happiness than that proportion, which that part of happiness bears to the happiness of his whole life; which two faults we usually term 'living fast and prodigally'.

6th Proposition

Such a man is more wise as he comes nearer the procuring of as much happiness as is worth 32 years and £4,940 and the more a fool as he comes short of procuring it.

Demonstration   This follows clearly from the 4th and 5th propositions.

1st Problem

How to express the value of such a man's time in money.

By the 4th postulate, the value of time may be expressed by a proportionable value in money. Therefore, since by the first proposition, the whole time of such a man is 32 years, and by the second proposition, his whole estate is £4,940, I make the following tables:

Table 1, expressing the value of such a man's time in money:

		£	s	d	f
1 year	worth	154	7	6	
1 month	worth	12	17	3	3
1 day	worth		8	5	2
1 hour	about			4	1
1 minute	near				3/10

Table 2 [on page 148] shows how much of such a man's money and time any year current from the beginning of the first period at postulate 5, to the last year does amount to; namely, 55.32 : : 1 year.

Note 1   This table is made necessary according to this proportion. As the whole time between the beginning of the first period and the end of his life, namely 55 years, is to his real time, namely, 32 years, so is one year to 212 days of his real time; and the value of it £89 16s. of his money or true estate.

Note 2   In this table months are omitted because they are either unequal in themselves, or bear no just proportion to time.

Lemma   That in the following propositions allowances must be made for the different inclinations and fancies of men and expectation of the world. But what is laid down determinately may now pass for a good general mean.

Years current	Years	Days	Hours	Mins.	Secs.	Whole days	£	s	d	f
1	0	212	12	13	5	512	89	16	7	3
2	1	059	18	26	10	425	179	13	3	2
3	1	272	6	39	16	637	269	9	11	1
4	2	119	12	52	21	850	359	6	7	
5	2	332	1	5	27	1062	449	3	2	3
6	3	179	7	18	32	1275	538	19	10	2
7	4	26	13	31	38	1487	628	16	6	1
8	4	239	1	44	43	1700	718	13	2	
9	5	86	7	57	48	1912	808	9	9	3
10	5	298	20	10	52	2125	898	6	5	2

7th Proposition
Such a man is a fool if he lay out upon what happiness may be included in the first period of the scheme. Postulate 5 above, 4 years and 26 days and 13 hours of his own time, and £628.16.4¼ of his money.

Demonstration   From the corollary of the 5th proposition, such a man is a fool if he lays out upon any particular and determinate part of the happiness of his whole life more of his 32 years and £4,940 than that part of his happiness has proportion to his whole happiness. But by the scheme at the 5th postulate, it appears that the happiness of the first period is answerable to 7 common years, and that by table 2 after problem 1, amounts to 4 years 26 days and 13 hours of his time and £628.16.6d of his money. Therefore such a man is a fool if he lays out upon the first period above 4 years 26 days and 13 hours of his time and above £628.16.6d of his money. *Q.E.D.*

8th Proposition
Such a man is a fool if he lays out upon the happiness of the second period above 5 years 86 days and 7 hours of his time, and £808.9.9¾d. of his money.
    The demonstration is the same as the 7th proposition.

148

9th Proposition

Or if he lays out upon the happiness of the third period above 6 years, 146 days, 8 hours of his time, and above £988.3.1¼d. of his money.

The demonstration is the same.

Table 3 A table showing what common money does amount to of such a man's money:

Common money	Such a man's money			
£	£	s	d	q
I		12	10	I
2	I	5	8	3
3	I	18	7	
4	2	11	5	2
5	3	14	3	3
6	3	17	2	I
7	4	10		2
8	5	2	11	
9	5	15	9	I
10	6	8	7	3
20	12	17	3	2
30	19	5	11	I
40	25	14	7	
50	32	3	2	3
60	38	11	10	2
70	45		6	I
80	51	9	2	
90	57	17	9	3
100	64	6	5	2
200	128	12	11	
300	192	19	4	2
400	257	5	10	
500	321	12	3	2
600	385	18	9	
700	450	5	2	2
800	514	11	8	
900	578	18	I	2
1000	643	4	7	

10th Proposition

Or, if he lays out on the 4th period above 7 years, 206 days, 2 hours of his time, and £1167.16.4¾d. of his money.
The demonstration is the same.

11th Proposition

Or, if on the last period above 8 years, 265 days, 21 hours of his time, and above £1,347.9.8d. of his money.
The same demonstration. [See Table 3.]

2nd Problem

How to express the real value of an acquired estate. If a man by the time he is 30 years of age, having discharged all debts and incumbrances, has by his labour acquired just £120 per annum and is to live to the age of 64 years, his real estate is £2,245.8.0d.

For £120 per annum during the following 34 years amounts to £2,245.8.0d., out of which by proposition 2, subtract:

		£	s	d
1	For charity	408		
2	For food, lodging, necessaries	292		
3	For clothes	252		
4	For expenses in sickness	72		
5	For the value of his time between the 9th and 30th year of his age, supposing that by the labour to acquire that estate 6 hours every day came to be not at his own disposal, by problem 2; about	810	12	

The sum of which deductions: £1834 12

Taken out of: £4080
The remainder is: £2245 8

Hence appears the true difference between an estate acquired and an estate that descends to one by inheritance. The time spent in acquiring of it, being converted into money, which in the above case is £810.12.0d.

3rd Problem

To apply the foregoing propositions to particular cases. For instance, by this method to find out the real value of an horse.

We proceed by these degrees:

1 We set down the man's age that is to buy the horse; suppose 33.

2 The period in which his age falls. How 'tis the third period.

3 The remainder of the money which the man has left to spend in the remainder of that period, which is then found. By the fifth postulate, the common years of the third period are 11, and by the ninth proposition, the money to be spent in these 11 years is £988. Therefore, since 8 years of the 11 are now supposed to be past, and 11 and 8 : : £988 and £718 (not troubling ourselves with fractions) which subduct the money already spent, namely, £718 out of £988 the whole, and the remainder will be £270 which is the sum that is at his disposal in those three years.

Another, and more compendious, way there is of finding it out by the 2nd Table where, over against three years we find £269.9.11d, between which and the £270, allowance being made for the fractions, the difference will be inconsiderable.

4 Suppose an indifferent horse and the market rate to be £10.

5 Suppose him, if no accident happens, to be serviceable for 10 years to come.

6 Suppose the yearly charge of keeping him to be £5. So the money to be laid out upon him will in effect be £60. It follows, therefore:

7 That the profit, pleasure and service that the horse must do to such a man, so that he may be no loser by him, must be worth of such a man's money £60 in 10 years; that is £6 per annum and consequently for the three years of the period in which the man then is, he must be worth £18 of his money (for 10 years, £60: 3 years, £18), and in the next period he must be worth £42, being the remainder, and therefore:

8 The man must consider what occasion he has for £270 in those three years, and whether he can wisely allow £18, being 1/15 of the value of the happiness of the 3 years for that horse. And whether he may allow it or no, he may find by the corollary of the 5th proposition.

If he finds that he must not allow so much, then by making subductions for what remains to be subducted, after taking out 14/15 from £270, the remainder will be the exact sum which he may afford for that horse. And that will be to that man the real value of it.

That is to say, if he finds, for instance, that besides £252 which is

14/15 of £270, he shall have occasion to lay out £10 upon other things, let him subduct the £262 from £270 and the remainder being £8 will be the true value of the horse to him.

After the same manner, the value of servant, books, garments, coach, *etc.*, may be found out.

Appendix B

[The extract from Descartes's *Of Method* which Aubrey attaches to his chapter on Logic (pp. 119–21) contains the now familiar statement of the philosopher's intellectual point of departure when, disillusioned by the education he had received at the Jesuit college at La Flêche, he determined to erase from his mind all that he had been taught, and to search for a new certainty. The *Discours de la Méthode* appeared in 1637 and was a prelude to the more exacting *Meditationes de Prima Philosophia*, 1641, and *Principia Philosophiae*, 1644. The four stages in the Cartesian method—doubt, analysis, the ordering of experience, and resolution—had a particular appeal for Aubrey, but for practical purposes he preferred that the students in his school should use Dr. Pell, whose 'ratiocination by syllogisms in his solutions to questions will teach logic beyond all other ways.']

Monsieur des Cartes, *Of Method*

Upon examination of them, I observed that, as for logic, its syllogisms and the greater part of its other rules, serve rather to expound to another the things they know, or even as Lulle's art, to speak with judgement of things we are ignorant of, than to learn them. And although, in effect, it contain divers most true and good precepts yet then are so many others mix't amongst them either hurtful or superfluous, that it's even as difficult to extract them as 'tis to draw a Diana, or a Mercury out of a lump of marble, which is not yet rough hewn.

—— For this reason, I thought I ought to seek some other method, which comprehending the advantages of these, they might be exempt from their defects. And as the multitude of laws often furnisheth excuses for vice, so a state is far better policed when having but a few, they are very strictly observed therein. So, instead of the great many precepts whereof logic is composed, I thought these four following would be sufficient for me, if I took but a firm and constant resolution not once to fail in the observation of them.

The first was, never to receive anything as true but what I evidently knew to be so; that is to say, carefully to avoid precipitation, and prevention, and to admit nothing more into my judgement but what should so clearly and distinctly present itself to my mind, that I could have no reason to doubt it.

The second, to divide every one of these difficulties which I was to examine, into as many parcels as could be, and was requisite, the better to resolve them.

The third, to lead my thoughts in order, beginning by the most simple objects, and the easiest to be known; to rise by little and little, as by steps even, to the knowledge of the most mix't, and even supposing an order amongst those which naturally do not preceed the other.

And the last, to make every such exact calculations and such general reviews that I might be confident to have omitted nothing.

Those long chains of reasons, though simple and easy, which the geometricians commonly use to lead us to their most difficult demonstrations, gave me occasion to imagine that all things which may fall under the knowledge of man, follow one another in the same manner, and so we do only abstain from receiving any one for true, which is not so, and observe always the right order of deducing them, one from the other. There can be none so remote to which at last we shall not attain, nor so hid, which we shall not discover. Neither was I much troubled to seek by which it behoved me to begin, for I already knew that it was by the most simple, and easiest to be discerned.

—— But considering that amongst all those who have formerly sought the truth in learning, none but the mathematicians only could find any demonstrations, that is to say any certain and evident reasons, I doubted not but that it was by the same that they have examined; although I did hope for no other profit but only that they would accustom my mind to nourish itself with truth and not content itself with reasons. But that which pleased me most in this method was the assurance I had, wholely to use my reason, if not perfectly, at least as much as it was in my power. Besides this, I perceived in the practice of it, my mind, by little and little accustomed itself to conceive its objects more clearly and distinctly; and having not subjected it to any particular matter, I proposed myself to apply it also as profitable to the difficulties of other sciences as I had to algebra. Not that I therefore durst at first undertake to examine all which might present themselves for that were contrary to the order it prescribes. But having observed that all their principles were to be borrowed from philosophy, in which I had found yet none that were ever certain, I thought it were needful for me in the first place to endeavour to establish some; and that this being the most important thing in the world, wherein precipitation and prevention were the most to be feared, I should not undertake to perform it till I had obtained a riper age than XXIII which was then mine. —— I was sensible of such extreme content since I began to use this method, that I thought none could in this life be capable of any more sweet and innocent and daily discovering, by means thereof some truths which seemed to me of importance, and commonly such as other men were ignorant of, the satisfaction I thereby received did so possess my mind, as if all things else concerned me not.

God having given to every one of us a light to discern truth from falsehood, I could not believe I ought to content myself one moment with opinions of others unless I had proposed to myself in due time to employ my judgement in the examination of them. Neither could I have exempted myself in scruple in following them, had I not hoped to lose no occasion of finding but better, if there were any.

But to conclude, I could not have bounded my desires, nor have been content, had I not followed a way whereby thinking myself assured to acquire all knowledge I could be capable of, I thought I might, by the same means, attain all that was truely good, which should ever be within my power; for as much as our will, inclining itself to follow or fly, nothing but what our understanding proposeth good, or ill, to judge well is sufficient to do well, and to judge the best we can, to do also what's best; to wit, to acquire all virtues, and with them all acquirable goods, and whosoever is sure of that, he can never fail of being content.

Appendix C

[Hartlib's preoccupation with language teaching and his association with the group of educational reformers who followed Bacon, Montaigne and William Bathe, the Irish Jesuit, has been noted elsewhere (see p. 164). It is interesting, in view of the current debate about the significance of Milton's *Of Education* and his apparent opposition to Commenian educational policies which Hartlib represented in England, that on this matter, at least, the two are in agreement. The sterility of current practices and the untimeliness of most Latin courses in schools which Milton criticizes here, resemble the 'grammatical tyranny of tongues' described by Hartlib in *The True and Ready Way*, 1654.

Aubrey inserts the extracts from Milton's letter after his chapter on Grammar (pp. 88–96).]

Mr. John Milton's letter to Mr. Sam. Hartlib, at the end of his poems. (The whole may be inserted.)

—— But because our understanding cannot in this body found itself but on sensible things, nor arrive so clearly to the knowledge of God, and things invisible, as by orderly conning over the visible and the inferior creature, the same method is necessarily to be followed in all discreet teaching. And seeing that every nation affords not experience and tradition enough for all kinds of learning, therefore we are chiefly taught the languages of those peoples who have at any time been most industrious after wisdom; so that language is but the instrument conveying to us things useful to be known. And though a linguist should pride himself to have all the tongues that Babel cleft the world into, yet if he had not studied the solid things in them as well as the words and lexicons, he were nothing so much to be esteemed a learned man as a yeoman, or a tradesman, competently wise in his mother dialect only. Hence appear the many mistakes which have made learning generally so unpleasing and so unsuccessful. First, we do amiss to spend seven or eight years merely in scraping together so much miserable Latin and Greek as might be otherwise learned easily and delightfully in one year.

—— for the usual method of teaching Arts, I deem it to be an old error of the universities not yet well recovered from the scholastic grossness of barbarian ages, that instead of beginning with Arts most easy (and those are such as are most obvious to the sense) they present their young, unmatriculated novices at first coming, with the most un-intellective abstractions of logic and metaphysics: so that they, having but newly left those grammatic flats and shallows where they stuck un-reasonably to learn a few words with lamentable construction, and now on a sudden transported under another climate to be toss'd and turmoil'd with their un-ballasted wits in fathomless and unquiet deeps of controversy, do, for the most part, grow into hatred and contempt of learning, mock'd and deluded all this while with ragged notions and babblements, while they expected worthy and delightful knowledge.

—— some allur'd to the trade of the law, grounding their purposes not on the prudent and heavenly contemplation of Justice and Equity (which was never taught them) but on the promising and pleasing thoughts of litigious terms, fat contentions, and flowing fees. Others betake them to state affairs with souls so un-principled in virtue and true generous breeding that flattery and courtships and tyrannous aphorisms appear to them the highest points of wisdom. [*Of Education.*]

Notes

Introduction

1 *Journals of the House of Lords 1578–1714*, 7 May 1662.
2 These trends are examined in detail by L. Stone in *The Crisis of the Aristocracy, 1558–1641*, 1965; T. Hollingworth in 'The Demography of the British Peerage', *Population Studies*, Supplement xviii, 1965; W. G. Hoskins in *Provincial England*, 1963, *et al.*
3 See F. Watson, *The Beginnings of the Teaching of Modern Subjects in England*, 1909; still the most complete examination of the origins of curricular studies.
4 See Anon. [R. Allestree?], *The Whole Duty of Man; The Ladies' Calling; The Causes of the Decay of Christian Piety*; I. Barrow's *Of Industry*; and Edward Veal's Sermon v, *Morning Exercises*, ii, 5.
5 Sermon x, *Morning Exercises at Cripplegate, St Giles in the Fields and in Southwark*, i, 194.
6 Aubrey's note, appended in the text to his description of the effects of training on innate ability. See p. 53.
7 Henry Wotton, *Essay on the Education of Children in the First Rudiments of Learning*, 1753; William Wotton, *Reflections on Ancient and Modern Learning*, 1694; Obadiah Walker, *Of Education, Especially of Young Gentlemen*, Oxford, 1673; Bathsua Makin, *Essay to Revive the Antient Education of Gentlewomen in Religion, Manners, Arts, and Tongues, with an Answer to the Objections against this way of Education*, 1673; Stephen Penton, *Guardian's Instruction, or the Gentleman's Romance*, 1688; Thomas Tryon, *New Methods of Educating Children*, 1695; Thomas Baker, *Reflections upon Learning*, 1700; Robert Ainsworth, *Most Natural and Easie way of Institution, Containing Proposals for making a Domestic Education less Chargeable to Parents and more Easie and Beneficial to Children*, 1698. Aubrey priced the publication costs of 500 copies. With

marginal notes, his *Idea* would have cost eleven shillings a sheet; without, ten.

8 Notably after the publication of A. Powell, *John Aubrey and His Friends*, 1948, and O. Lawson Dick, *John Aubrey's Brief Lives*, 1949.

Chapter 1 Proem

1 In fact, the Mathematical School was added to the Hospital in 1673. It had the support of Newton, Pepys and Halley, and the promise of £1,000 a year for seven years from the King. It was one of several attempts at that time to make good the critical shortage of mathematicians and navigators which was believed to be a threat to national security.

2 In 1638, presumably, when Blandford was under a William Sutton, whose father of the same name must have had the school. The elder Sutton died in 1632 when Aubrey was six years old. The son was possibly usher to William Gardiner, master to 1636, whom Aubrey names elsewhere as his first schoolmaster.

Chapter 2 The Institution

1 Aubrey inserts a note at this point, 'Dr. Burnet, *de hiis*'. Gilbert Burnet's *Thoughts on Education* was written *c.* 1668 but published only in 1761. See J. Clarke, *Bishop Gilbert Burnet as an Educationist*, 1914. H. C. Foxcroft's *Supplement to Burnet's History of My Own Time* describes at length the methods Burnet followed (with modest success) in the education of his three sons, William, Gilbert and Thomas.

2 From 1663 to 1666.

3 Canonbury House, Islington (built by Sir John Spencer, Lord Mayor of London during Elizabeth's reign, and a Levant merchant) much admired and copied. More recently, the plaster-work of its ceilings has been used as a model for the new ceilings in Fountains Hall, Ripon.

4 Oxford had other disadvantages. There were, according to Aubrey, four or five boarding schools for young gentlewomen there in 1678, as well as other less reputable establishments. 'This is to put fire and flax together, and several young heirs and gentlemen commoners have split upon this rock.'

5 Aubrey cites Milton's letter to Hartlib: 'I call a complete and generous education that which fits a man to perform justly, skilfully and magnanimously all the offices, both private and public, of peace and war, which may be done between twelve and one and twenty.' [*Of Education.*]

Chapter 3 Government

1 As proof of this Aubrey recounts the experience of Hobbes. 'Mr. Hobbes told me that G., Duke of Buckingham at Paris when he was about XX years old desired him to read geometry. His Grace had great natural parts and quickness of wit. Mr. Hobbes read, and his Grace did not apprehend, which Mr. Hobbes wondered at. At length Mr. Hobbes observed that his Grace was at masturbation—his hand in his codpiece. That is a very improper age for that reason for learning.'

2 Aubrey's note: '*Aurora musis amica*—not a general rule for all men, but for no children; for their rising betimes dwarfs them and spoils their growth. For the chief time of perspiration is in the morning, as also the time of assimilation, and sleep concocts and digests their phlegm. Wherefore, for everyone for the hour of rising the statera is to be consulted with. But how contrary the course was at Blandford School and other schools. At six o'clock in the morning in Mr. Gardiner's time, which shortened his life and jaded his scholars. And for my part, for want of perspiration, I did nothing but gape an hour or two, the tears running down abundantly as if I had wept, which tears should have perspired. Who constantly rises before the work of perspiration is ended, insensibly destroys himself, shortening his days by dropsey or asthma. Well may one to to plough or thrash so early, the robustness of the exercise making compensation. But to read awakening as a sleeper will turn to little account. Apollo winds not his horn to call the Muses till these fogs are vanished. Who makes verses does very well know this for a truth.'

Chapter 4 Relaxation and Bodily Exercise

1 Aubrey's *Idea* is remarkable for its neglect of physical education, for after the publication of Elyot's *Gouvernour* and Castiglione's *Cortegiano* it was usual for those who wrote on the education of the nobility—Peacham, Durie, Milton, *inter al.*—to devote some space to training bodily skills. Aubrey seems to have settled for the paradigm of the scholarly English country gentleman.

2 Presumably the section on plants in *Catalogus Plantarum Angliae*, 1670, which Ray undertook with Francis Willughby.

3 The Real Character was a form of logical symbolism applied to language. It depended on a meticulous and exhaustive classification of human thought and experience similar in form to the *Thesaurus* of P. M. Roget. Unfortunately, it required not only a prodigious memory but it was unable to accommodate the rapid expansion of scientific thought and the advances in experimental knowledge which were then taking place. It seemed to Aubrey, however, to have unlimited potential as a universal

written language. See J. Wilkins's *An Essay towards a Real Character and a Pholosophical Language*, 1668.

4 Though not acknowledged, the emphasis on the practical value of agriculture and husbandry is in the tradition of Hartlib and his associates during the Commonwealth period. For they publicized the utility of these studies and encouraged specialization. It has been suggested that the professionalism William Browne and Cressy Dymock brought to these aspects of natural science led to their disappearance from the schools. Clearly, by this time gentlemanly study of trees and flowers as an adjunct of heraldry was no longer fashionable.

5 Aubrey's note: 'Let 'em make, as they do rusticate, a *Hortus Strius* or *Real Herbal*, which will be a nest-egg and allure them more and more.' The *adversaria* in which information would be collected was a pocket note-book or journal.

6 The art of judging character and disposition from the features of the face had a special appeal for Aubrey. As a primer in physiognomy he recommends Camillo Baldi's *Commentarii in Aristotelis Physiognomica*.

7 Aubrey's note: 'A course in chemistry may be run through in four weeks at the Museum in Oxford, of great use both in cities and countries, *sc.* to make one's own medicines. For example, that eminent and able and learned physician, Sir Theodore de Mayern, when a patient addressed himself to him, his apothecary in the first place made enquiry what his estate was; next, if he were a married man; and they would use a conscience accordingly. Thus, by this sad example one may see how useful a thing it is to understand a little of physick, and to be able to make one's own medicines. And not only upon account of the charge, which is considerable, but for one's own health, safety and preservation. Besides, in the country there is no way else. I have heard that eminent and learned Dr. Ridgeley, who is a saint as well as a great physician and chemist, say that did the people know the knavery of their profession, not to speak of their ignorance, they would throw stones at 'em in the streets.'

8 Gleek, a card-game for three, and the two versions of primero, a Spanish game played with a pack of forty cards, were popular gambling games in Tudor and Stuart times.

Chapter 6 The Cursus

1 The success of the school course, the attitudes scholars adopted to their studies and to the world at large, were to a great extent determined by their early experiences. From the jottings in various parts of the manuscript Aubrey seems to have intended to give some space to early childhood in this context. Of the writers who influenced him, Keckerman and Pierre Charron are the most notable. For example, the notion that the

temperature of the seed of the parents determined the disposition of the child at birth is to be found in Charron, as is the doctrine of transpiration—the idea that young children are like sponges, capable of absorbing both the good and the harmful influences of their environment. 'How can it be,' Aubrey asked, 'but when a pretty infant lies with a great, filthy, black-groined, ill-term'd jade, but that he mingles her poisonous vapours in his body?' But if she were young, 'clear of skin, of a kindly smell, pure complexion, of good temperature, wholesome and of moderate diet, much sleep, little anger, neither too idle nor too toyling; no wine-bibber, no eater of spices, no ordinary wanton and void of all diseases', then the upbringing of the young child could be safely left in her hands. Parents then would do well to examine carefully the wet nurse they hired for their children. If they heeded his admonitions they would test the quality of her milk: it should be 'neither blue-transparent nor grey, but white, sweet yet not in excess, which causes scabs and sharpness of urine'. The dry nurse would be 'a wench of sweet nature and of a very healthy complexion; brown hair or chestnut ... a sweet natured eye, the most comfortable object in the world to the spirits; not a fiery eye, nor a witch-like black eye, nor a gib-cat spiteful eye, but a very good-natured hazel.'

2 Aubrey's note: 'Tis strange and a thing not to be touched at, what influence sweet or ill aspects have on tender infants, especially those of the most tender and delicate brains and spirits. ——has analysed it down to his infancy and well remembers it. Mr. T. B. [Thomas Bushell, possibly. See A. Powell, *John Aubrey and his Friends*, 36, 236] would not only not let a servant give any child of his a hard word, but also they durst not give them a hard look; which was done like a wise man. Nor will a wise father but order that his servants shall be obedient to his children—the good or ill consequence keeping up, or breaking or debasing their spirits, making them companions for serving men who make it their artifice to gain ascendency over heirs. Sir John Danvers was wont to tell me that the only virtue of travel in those days was to wean their sons from the acquaintance of serving men.'

3 See A. Wood, *Athenae Oxonienses*, ed. P. Bliss, vol. 2 (1815), 671. During the Interregnum he was a fellow of the newly erected college at Durham and after 1660, when it was dissolved, became a private schoolmaster at a house belonging to Sir Thomas Fisher in Islington. He invented a method of teaching children to write a good hand in twenty days by copying over in black ink letters printed in red from copper plates. Tonge also opened an academy for girls before being charged with complicity in the Popish Plot.

4 The text-pen was used on the continent, particularly in Holland, to teach children to write the large, flowing text-hand.

5 Nor did the schools apparently take account of the fact that October and February were the best months for study. Aubrey's note: 'Mr. Edward

Philips, nephew and amanuensis to his uncle, Mr. John Milton when he wrote his *Paradise Lost*, told me that his uncle's wit did flow most in those two months; in mid-summer and mid-winter with difficulty.' And, regarding October and February, 'Lord Bacon in his *Advancement of Learning*—your young men shall see visions and your old men dream dreams.'

6 Aubrey's note: 'Note Mr. North's advantage of his tutor making him perfectly to understand what he read before he left him. This must be done in grammar teaching, it being the basis.'

7 In his general description of courses of study, Aubrey makes no mention of shorthand. It had penetrated the schools after the Reformation when it became fashionable to take notes of the sermons of the early protestant preachers whose works were rarely published. Peter Bales (1547–1610) commended it in *The Writing Schoolmaster* as a method of enabling scholars 'to write as a man speaketh, treatably'. Aubrey, in one of the addenda, wondered whether they 'should learn shorthand. For example, that of Willis or Shelton—which is the best (Mr. Abraham Hill says Willis's)—or whether the Real Character may not serve their turn in this. As to the writing of sermon notes, I would not trouble them, because the way before proposed is better. But shorthand is of great use for lawyers for taking reports and unless it is to be learned when boys it will not be serviceable. Besides it will be useful in their private *adversaria*.' Willis's shorthand had been superseded by that of Jeremiah Rich (*The Pen's Dexterity*, 1646) and was in general use by theological students and senior schoolboys in the second half of the seventeenth century.

Chapter 9 School Exercises

1 Short sentences containing worthy precepts and exhortations to students to be of good behaviour.

Chapter 11 Grammar

1 Reform of grammar teaching was one of Aubrey's principal objectives. He was anxious to get away from the arid and often brutal methods which were widely employed. Moreover, he saw that a reduction in the time spent learning Latin, and to a lesser extent Greek, could be usefully turned to the advantage of mathematics and the sciences. Hence his approval of the changes advocated by Bacon, Montaigne and Lubinus. There is some evidence also that he sympathized with the small group of reformers who were at that time questioning the whole basis of language teaching, which involved more than support for the vernacular or the

search for an acceptable Latin style. Their discussions centred on the nature of language and concepts, learning strategies and motivation. Hooke evidently, in Aubrey's view, had seen the significance of the current debate. For a full discussion of this movement see C. Webster, *Samuel Hartlib and the Advancement of Learning*, 1970, 17–21.

2 Aubrey's note: '*An Introduction to the Latin Tongue*, by Israel Tonge, D.D. Mr. Lewis of Tottenham, near London, schoolmaster, was Dr. Tonge's acquaintance and has the key to the anigmatical part of these verses.'

3 Aubrey's note: 'Erasmus in his book *De Conferendis Epistolis* would not have them to spend much time in construing and parsing, but touch only at the past-perfect tenses and supines, or some such remarkable instance.'

4 Aubrey's note: 'Let them double translate Pliny's *Panegyric* and then compare it with the translation of Mr. White Kennet, London, 1686. Quintilian's *Declamations* are, they say, well translated into English lately at Mr. Hensman's in Westminster Hall. *The Oration for Marcus Marcellus* by M. T. Cicero translated into English, 1689, at Mr. Kettleby's in St. Paul's churchyard.'

5 Aubrey's opinion was that at that critical age boys should not be introduced to Martial's (scandalous) *Epigrams* or *Journals*. The Greek of Appian, however, was another matter. It had the advantage of being comprehensible to those whose vocabulary was limited to about 200 words, and it was invaluable in implanting a sense of history. Herodian, too, was 'good Greek, and very good history'.

6 Aubrey's note: 'Ovid's *Metamorphoses*, translated by G. Sandys: this will please their tender fancies and insensibly lull them asleep into the love of reading. It is Englished grammatically by —— Hall, at Mr. Starkey's, one shilling. Also it is translated by —— Brinsley grammatically; as also is Virgil. Mr. John Ogilby's translation of Homer's *Iliad* and *Odyssey*.'

7 Joseph Webbe was the centre of the group of educationists referred to above. He appears to have had the support of Thomas Horne who taught at Leicester, Tonbridge and Eton, and Thomas Hayne, a master at Christ's Hospital. His book, *An Appeale to Truth, In the Controversie between Art and Use; about the best and most expedient Course of Languages*, 1622, was a radical departure from standard methods. It dispensed entirely with grammatical rules and relied on an ingenious system of double translation.

8 Aubrey's note: 'See Corderius's *Instructions for Teaching Children Latin* before his translation of the *Select Epistles of Cicero;* to which annex the advice of Ludovicus Vives on the same subject. And Mr. Roger Ascham's *Schoolmaster*; he also wrote a grammar which I could never yet light upon.'

Chapter 12 Mathematics

1 Though the teaching of mathematics to the young had had advocates for a century or more when Aubrey began compiling his notes for the *Idea*, it had made little impact in the grammar schools. Most of the energies of grammar school masters went into the teaching of the classics, and such mental discipline as was thought necessary was imparted, not in arithmetic or geometry, but in dialectic. Much of the advanced teaching of the subject was done by private individuals, even in Aubrey's time. Dr. Robert Recorde, whose *Ground of Arts*, *Pathway to Knowledge*, *Castle of Knowledge* and *Whetstone of Wit* place him in a high position among writers on mathematics in the later sixteenth century, was not a teacher in an academic institution. Nor were John Speidell, John Kersey or John Ward, whom Aubrey cites.

Like Bacon, Aubrey saw mathematics as mental gymnastic—'if the wit be too dull (the mathematics) sharpen it; if too wandering, they fix it; if too inherent in sense, they abstract it'—but his appreciation of the work of Descartes and Newton led him to the view that it would also offer in its higher forms the basis of mechanical philosophy. In the narrower sense mathematics—both the arithmetic of the pen or 'cyphering', and the casting of accounts—had immediate practical value for those who were to be leaders in society and managers of estates. The lively interest Aubrey took in the subject and his wide knowledge of contemporary mathematical texts are the more remarkable since he, like several of his associates in the Royal Society, came to the subject late.

2 Aubrey's note: 'The learned Leonard Digges, Esq., his father taught him arithmetic when he was a child. Also, John Dee assisted him when he was a child; both which appears by Mr. Digges in the Preface to his *Atlas*.' Digges, a member of parliament and muster-general of the English forces in the Netherlands, was the author of *Tectonicon*, 1556, *Pantometria*, 1571, and *Stratioticos*, 1579.

3 Aubrey's note: 'Let them have Mr. Spiedell's collection of 80 questions in common arithmetic, with their answers, 8°.'

4 The origin of casting out nines is uncertain. The Roman mathematician Hippolytus used the process in the third century, and it appears in the works of the Italian, Fibonacci, c. 1202, and in Robert Recorde's *Ground of Arts* in 1540. For this, as for other aspects of mathematics teaching in its historical context, see *Historical Topics for the Mathematics Classroom*, National Council for Mathematics, Washington, 1969.

5 Aubrey's note: '*Quare*, Mr. Wyn, the mathematical instrument maker, if amongst John Collin's papers there is not his excellent method of household accounts for Charterhouse. He gave one to me to deliver to my Lord Keeper North and another for myself is left at Mr. Ashmole's.'

6 Aubrey's note: 'Alderman Gambleton of London told me that Colonel

Alexander Popham, who had £9,000 per annum, was wont to make his complaints of casting up of long bills of accounts, which terrified him, and many times he looked [only] at the foot of the account.' Aubrey's own unfortunate financial experiences explain the incredulity with which he viewed such cavilier behaviour.

7 A memorandum to the author: 'Get Mr. J. Ward, his way of the *Rule of Practice*, shorter than any tradesman's, or common arithmetic; *Arithmetical Common Questions*, by Euclid Spiedell at Mr. Leos, the globemaker in the Poultrey, 8º; *Foster's Arithmetic* by Mr. Henry Coley, very plain.'

8 Seth, Lord Bishop of Sarum, and Lord John Vaughan were in Aubrey's opinion the only two persons he knew who understood it.

9 Aubrey intended to approach Robert Hooke 'for his engine for speedy division and immediate finding out the divisor. And inquire about performing it by a line of numbers.'

10 Aubrey added, under the title of *The Royal Almanack*, 1678, the following:

> I have, out of my mathematical compendium, which will shortly be printed with addition, added a table which is of constant use, to know the price of either the near, or the great, hundred, which is 112^l, at any small rate the pound weight.* The first column contains the price of one pound from one farthing to two shillings, and in the second you have the price of the hundredweight. The greater figures are pence; the lesser, farthings. If the price exceed the table, take a half or a quarter of it, and double or redouble the price. So, seeking in the table the price of a hundredweight, you have the price of a pound.
>
> For example. At 3½d the pound, what comes either hundredweight to?
>
> Put the price of a pound into farthings, *viz*. 14. For the near hundred, account twice so many shillings and as many pence as farthings; and for the greater hundred, twice so many shillings and as many groats as there be farthings in the pound weight. For example, 14/– and 14/– make 28/–, and 14d. makes 29/2 the near hundred. And 14/– twice and 14 groats makes 32/8 for the great hundred. So daily expenses are for every penny spent a day, one pound, one half pound, one groat, one penny. 5d. a day is, after that rate, £7 12s. 1d.

Chapter 13 Geometry

1 Aubrey's note: 'Dr. Seth Ward, now Bishop of Sarum, when he was President of Trinity College, Oxford, did draw his geometrical schemes

* The near hundredweight contained 100 pounds; the great, or long, hundredweight, 112 pounds.

in black, red, yellow, green, and blue ink to avoid perplexity of A, B, C, etc. Dr. Pell told me of a learned divine, a German whose name I have forgot, that did use inks of diverse colours, e.g., black, red, yellow, green, blue, and that he did find benefit by it for his memory's sake.'

2 The pre-Copernican astronomy contained in the *Almagest* was perhaps less important to Aubrey than its mathematical techniques, for it included plane and spherical trigonometry, tables of chords, and a table of natural series, which formed the basis of time-measurement and of calculations of distance on land and sea.

3 In emphasizing the practical value of geometry, Aubrey is restating a point of view which receives full expression in Henry Peacham's *The Compleat Gentleman*, 1622. It is concerned with the 'forms and draughts of all figures, greatness of all bodies, all manner of measures and weights, the cunning working of all tools; with all artificial instruments whatsoever. All engines of war . . . exosters, sambukes, catapults, testudoes, scorpions, petards, grenades, great ordinances of all sorts. By the benefit likewise of geometry, we have our goodly ships, galleys, bridges, mills . . . roofs and arches . . . clocks, curious watches, kitchen jacks, even the wheelbarrow.'

4 And not only in military matters. Aubrey includes here a marginal note from Robert Anderson's *Cut the Rigging*. 'Certainly, it may be taken as a general rule that the more any person is knowing in mathematics, the fitter he is for all parts of military affairs; and likewise a nation never receives greater damage and disgrace than when ignorant and unfaithful persons are put in places of trust, which I never wish to see in England whilst I am.'

5 The value of illustrations as aids to understanding in school books had been demonstrated by Lubinus in his *Epistolary Discourse*, annexed to *The True and Ready Way to Learn the Latin Tongue* which Hartlib edited in 1654, and by Comenius. Only during the Interregnum did it become widely recognized that drawing could be used to sharpen the observation and insight of children, notably by Petty, Snell and Dury. Aubrey himself set great store by painting and sketching. At eight years of age, he says, 'I fell then to drawing and at nine, crossed by father and schoolmaster, to colours, having nobody to instruct me, copied pictures.'

6 Aubrey's notes: 'As to portraiture, there is printed at Paris, 1688, *The Sentiment of the King of France's Painters, for the best rules and directions of drawing*, which let be practised by these youths whose geniuses incline them that way.'

'―― Wray, Esq., an extraordinary handsome man, paints very well for a gentleman, was taken prisoner by the Turks and carried to Algeria where he did maintain himself by painting their ships.'

7 Bugy (or Bougie, now Bejaia) was a fortified seaport in Algeria, a base from which the corsair pirates preyed upon Levant shipping.

8 Dialling—gnomonics—the art of constructing dials and measuring time

—appears in the prospectuses of several private teachers of mathematics. Both Speidell and Kersey, to whom Aubrey refers elsewhere in the text, offered to teach the art in their academies in Queen Street and in Charles Street, near the Piazza in Covent Garden.

9 Aubrey had it from Mr. Smythwick of the Royal Society that 'Clavius, his *Euclid*, is prolix and tedious; yet it has this use that when you come to a knot, he will certainly untie it.' Barrow's *Euclid* 'does not teach them to demonstrate'. For this reason, Sir Charles Scarborough made his son translate the Greek Euclid's demonstrations into Latin.

Chapter 15 Logic

1 For the intellectual content of the gentleman's education see G. C. Brauer, *The Education of a Gentleman: Theories of Gentlemanly Education in England, 1660–1775*, New York, 1959.

2 *ignorati elenchi*—a mode of argument by which an opponent's case seems to have been effectively demolished, but which on close examination refutes another case altogether. Further to this Aubrey recommends Griffith Powell 'who writes best of the fallacies'.

3 Aubrey's note: '[Dethlevus] Cluverus says he believes it is now printed to his *Logic*, which *quare*.'

4 Aubrey is not explicit about the Summulists but is evidently referring to the followers of Peter of Spain (Petrus Hispanus, or Juliani), the terminist logician, 1210–77. His *Summulae Logicales* was a standard textbook in the logic curriculum in the fourteenth and fifteenth centuries and ran into 150 printed editions. The texts of Petrus, containing many mnemonic devices, were known to Aubrey, as were the works of the logician William of Sherwood. In a note Aubrey recalls that Sir Charles Scarborough says 'that he found out how Aristotle found out his rules, which the schoolmen put into verses, *viz.*, Barbara, celarent, Darii, etc.' These mnemonics which designate the first, second and third moods of the first syllogistic figure, occur in Sherwood's *Introductiones in Logicam* where he deals with syllogisms.

5 Aubrey's note: 'There is a book in 8° *Of the Fallacies* by one Goveanus of Dublin College, printed about 1694. I guess it may be a pretty book.'

6 Evidence as to the value of a systematic mathematical training for training the logical faculties of the mind is added in the form of extracts from William Oughtred's *Clavis Mathematicae* which Aubrey inserts at this point.

Chapter 16 Rhetoric

1 Aubrey thought it would be good exercise for them to translate the Latin into English and then to compare with *Quintilian's Declamations, translated and attested by several schoolmasters about London*, 8°. Further, he cites Juvenal, *Satires, VI, Dic, dic aliquem sodes hic, Quintiliane, colorem.*

2 A reference to the practice in Tudor and Stuart times of inscribing on folded paper the name of the person to be drawn by lot as a lover or special friend for the ensuing year.

3 Regarding prose style, Aubrey recommends Sir Roger L'Estrange's *Aesop's Fables* which 'would not only be a delightful book for youths to read but it would open their understanding and teach them to write a clear and gentle style.'

4 Aubrey's note: 'Dr. Newton's *Art of Rhetoric*; Cicero Redivivus, at the Peacock and Bible in Paul's churchyard, 1688, teaches in short the rules of rhetoric.' Between the ages of 20 and 30—'in that rutting stage of life'—they might still be enticed by the works of Onuphrius Panvinius and Mercurialis. (Onofrio Panvinio, *Fastorum libri v a Romulo rege*; Hieronymous Mercurialis, *De Arte Gymnastica libri sex, in quibus exercitatiroum . . . vetustarum genera et quidquid denique ad corporis humani.*)

Chapter 17 Civil Law

1 The traditional antipathy of the upper classes for the universities obliged Aubrey to draw up a detailed scheme of training in the law, for most of his scholars would spend some time at the Inns of Court. Knowledge of the law, and of history, were thought to be suitable accomplishments for the gentleman, whether or not he entered government or the legal profession. Burnet, for example, considered that without an understanding of the law a man was 'but a poor nobleman'. But equally, the seventeenth century Inns of Court were expensive finishing schools, not very different from those of the early fifteenth century described in Selden's translation of *de Laudibus Legum Angliae*, where martial skills and the social graces were developed.

2 Aubrey's note: '*Processus juris brevissimis versibus, redditus a Sebastiano Scheffero*, Aldenberghensi Francafurti, 1572; an octavo about the bigness of Gadbury's *Almanack*. I saw it opposite to Gray's Inn. In iambic verses.'

3 Synderisis, or synterisis. Conscience, or that part of conscience which serves as a guide to right conduct.

4 Aubrey here advocates the setting up of a Land Registry to protect titles to land and to facilitate conveyancing. The idea of a Registry was popular with reformers both before and after the Restoration. Such an institution would have provided not only the machinery for the easier transfer of

land, but a convenient means of assessment for taxation. Since it was regarded as a Puritan measure, it found little favour after 1660 and has been only recently introduced.

5 It seems to have been Aubrey's intention to include in the *Idea* some solutions to easy law cases devised by Peyton Chester of Bedfordshire, 'brother of Sir Anthony Chester, one of the gentlemen of the Bedchamber to his Grace the Duke of Gloucester'. Peyton used 'the algebraical method of Mr. Descartes'. But he died, and Aubrey was 'forced to make a chasm here with a sigh: the death of my dear and honoured friend, Mr. Peyton Chester who died at Huntington on his return from Luffenham to London, September 27th, 1686. He was there buried in ——— Now since it has pleased God to take him, that learned and truely virtuous gentleman, I know not anyone in England that can, at present, perform this essay. There was one, Mr. Hammond of Gray's Inn, a K.C., a Kentish gentleman, that understood algebra: he told me that he found great use of it in solution of cases, but he also is dead.'

Chapter 19 Mundane Prudence

1 Prudential advice in the courtesy books of the Renaissance, derived largely from classical authors, implied a code of conduct based on heroic personal qualities, public service and patriotism. By the mid-seventeenth century these ideals had been largely superseded by a Christian code which placed emphasis more on piety and godliness: typical of these were R. Braithwaite's *The English Gentleman*, 1630, Richard Allestree's *The Gentleman's Calling*, 1660, and Clement Ellis's *Gentile Sinner*, 1660. Though Puritan in tone, their authors had widely different religious beliefs. A common factor was their insistence on honesty, charity, and good works and, after the Restoration, on modesty and humility, especially about ancestors and wealth. At the same time there was a continuing tradition of advice books which were cynical and worldly-wise, like Raleigh's *Instructions to his Sonne, and to Posterity*, 1632, and Du Refuge's *Traite de la Cour*, translated 1622, which advocated the study of men's prevailing weaknesses and the most expedient means of self-preservation and advancement. Chesterfield's letters to his son, a century later, epitomize this trend. In Aubrey one may detect both the Christian and the mundane.

2 They could do no better, Aubrey thought, than follow the advice of Erasmus in this matter, and he cites the first paragraph of the *Colloquies* to support his case.

3 Aubrey's note: 'See Justus Turceus, *de Lusu Aleae*, where he proves it is a disease and to be cured by physic; and that it proceeds from pride and that the Spaniards, the proudest nation, are most addicted to it. A very little book.'

Biographical Notes

Abingdon, James Bertie, Earl of. He was kinsman and patron of Aubrey and related by the marriage of Mary Bertie to Aubrey's friend, Anthony Henley. In 1696, when Edward Castle published Aubrey's *Miscellanies* it was dedicated to the Earl, then Lord Chief Justice in Eyre of the Royal Forests in the south of England. He was the brother of Aubrey's friend Captain Charles Bertie.

Agricola, Georgius, 1494–1555. The German mineralogist born in Saxony, whose *De Re Metallica*, 1530, is a compendium of technical and industrial processes.

Ainsworth, Robert, 1660–1743. Lexicographer, numismatist and teacher at schools in Bolton, Bethnal Green and Hackney. In addition to his educational treatise, he compiled a Latin–English dictionary, published in 1736.

Allestree, Richard, 1619–81. A royalist, expelled from Oxford during the Civil War. He was Regius Professor of Divinity, 1663–79, the author of *The Whole Duty of Man* and other improving tracts and sermons.

Alstead (Alsted), J. H., 1588–1638. His *Encyclopoedia scientiarium omnium* was published in 1630.

Alvarus, Emmanuel. The author of a number of Latin texts. His *Prosodia* was published in 1671, *An Introduction to the Latin Tongue* in 1686 and *Grammatica* in 1687.

Anderson, Robert. Author of works on gunnery and mathematics. *Cut the Rigging; and proposals for the Improvement of Great Artillery* was published in 1691. He died about 1696.

Aphrodisaeus, Alexander. Born at Aphrodisias towards the end of the second century, a peripatetic philosopher regarded as one of the principal exponents of Aristotle.

Apollinarius of Laodicea. The fourth-century theologian and logician.

Appian (Appianus). Second-century historian from Alexandria who compiled a history of Rome.

Argolus, Andreas. Mathematician and astronomer in the mid-seventeenth century. He wrote commentaries on the hypotheses of Tycho Brahe and on the Arab astronomers.

Aristarchus. The Greek grammarian and critic who edited Homer, Hesiod, Pindar, Aeschylus and Sophocles. He died about 150 B.C.

Ascham, Roger, 1515–68. He followed William Grindal as tutor to the Princess Elizabeth and served for a time as Latin secretary to Queen Mary. In the 1550s he held office at Cambridge University and was a prebendary of York. His unfinished educational treatise, *Scholemaster*, was published two years after his death.

Ashley, first Baron Anthony Ashley Cooper, 1621–83. The title was created in 1661.

Ashmole, Elias, 1617–92. The antiquary, lawyer and astrologer who held several minor posts in government after 1660. His collection of rarities, left to him by John Tradescant, were bequeathed to Oxford University and became the nucleus of the Ashmolean Museum.

Ax, Thomas. The servant and estate manager of Sir William Portman and Aubrey's friend. He died in 1691 and bequeathed £1,000 to encourage mathematical investigations into true longtitude for the benefit of navigators.

Aylmer, Brabazon. Bookseller, 1670–1709, at the Three Pigeons, near the Royal Exchange. He dealt mainly in theological works.

Bachet, Claude Gaspar. The French translator of the works of Diophantus, 1621. He also wrote a life of Aesop and compiled a collection of his fables.

Baker, Thomas. A popular writer on mathematics in the mid-seventeenth century. A catalogue of his mathematical works was published in 1683. In 1684 he published *Clavis geometrica catholica* and *Geometrical key*.

Baldi, Camillo, 1547–1634. Born at Bologna where his father was a professor of philosophy. He also held a chair of philosophy in the same university.

Balzac, Jean Louis Guez de, 1594–1654. An original member of the Academy, much admired for his model prose style.

Barbett, Paul. His *Praxis of physic*, first published in 1675, enjoyed great success at the time Aubrey was writing, and ran into several editions.

Barrow, Isaac, Bishop of Asaph, 1614–80. The Royalist divine who was expelled from his fellowship at Cambridge during the Civil War. He was made Bishop of Sodor and Man in 1663 and of Asaph in 1669.

Bathurst, Ralph, 1620–1704. A cleric and physician who sympathized with the King's cause but served during the Civil war in parliament's navy. He was chaplain to Charles II in 1663 and became president of Trinity College.

Bathurst, Theodore. Nephew of Ralph Bathurst. Latin poet and translator.
Baudius, Dominicus. The *Dominicii Baudii . . . Epistolarium centuriae tres* was published in 1620.
Baxter, Richard, 1615–91. The presbyterian divine.
Baynard, George, 1649–93. Son of Thomas Baynard of Clift, Dorset, who lived at Tincleton in the same county.
Beard, Thomas. A puritan divine and justice of the peace for Huntingdonshire. He was the author of a number of religious works, including *The Theatre of God's Judgements*. He died in 1632.
Becmannus (Becmann), Johann Christopher. The German historian and bibliographer who wrote in the last quarter of the seventeenth century.
Bergerac, Cyrano de, 1619–55. Poet and duellist.
Berkshire, Countess of. Presumably Elizabeth Cecil, daughter of William Cecil, Lord Burghley, second Earl of Exeter who married, 1621, Thomas Howard, first Earl of Berkshire.
Bettinus, Marius. His *Apiaria universae philosophiae* was published in 1642, his *Aerarium philosophiae mathematicae* in 1648.
Billingsley, Sir Henry. Lord Mayor of London, 1596. His *Euclid; the elements of geometry*, the first translation into English, appeared in 1570. He died around 1604.
Blaeu, William Janszoon, 1571–1638. The Dutch mathematician, geographer and astronomer who founded a publishing firm in Amsterdam which specialized in maps and atlases.
Blunderville (Blundeville), Thomas. The polymath writer on horsemanship, government, logic, astronomy and education. He was the first English writer to introduce plane trigonometry in his *Exercises* of 1594.
Boethius, Anicius Manlius Severinus. His life straddled the fifth and sixth centuries. He translated Aristotle's works and wrote on logic, arithmetic, music and theology.
Bradshaw, John, 1602–59. Regicide; parliamentary commissioner and president of the court for the trial of Charles I. In 1660, together with Cromwell, Ireton and Pride, his body was exhumed and hanged at Tyburn.
Brancker (Branker), Thomas, 1633–76. The mathematician, headmaster of Macclesfield grammar school and rector of Malpas. His *Doctrinae sphericae adumbratio* was published in 1662.
Brereton, Lord William, of Leaghlin in Ireland. M.P. for Cheshire and one of the founders of the Royal Society.
Bridgeman, Sir Orlando, 1606–74. Lord Keeper, 1667–72.
Briggs, Henry, 1561–1630. Mathematician and professor of geometry at Gresham College, London, 1596–1620.
Bringhurst, John. A bookseller and printer in Gracechurch Street near Cornhill, 1680–4. He was one of the few printers who dealt in Quaker books.

Brinsley, John. Master of the school at Ashby-de-la-Zouch around 1610. He was ejected in 1620 for his religious views. A translator and writer on education, his *Ludus literarius; or, the grammar schoole* is an excellent commentary on contemporary teaching methods (1612).

Broome, Henry, 1641–81. Printer and bookseller, succeeded in business by his widow Joanna.

Browne, Thomas, 1604–73. Archbishop Laud's chaplain, 1637.

Browne, William, 1628–78. Botanist and fellow of Magdalen College, Oxford.

Buckingham, George Villiers, second Duke of, 1628–87.

Burgherdicius (Burgersdijk, Franco. Writer on logic and philosophy in the mid-seventeenth century. His principal work, *Idea philosophae tum moralis*, was published in 1641.

Burghley, William Cecil, Lord, 1520–98. The alternative subject of Aubrey's anecdote. (See Salisbury.)

Burnet, Gilbert, Bishop of Salisbury, 1643–1715.

Busby, Richard, 1606–95. Headmaster of Westminster School, 1638–95, prebendary of Westminster and canon of Wells, one of the outstanding schoolmasters of the seventeenth century.

Bushell, Thomas, 1594–1674. Francis Bacon's page. Later an eccentric mineralogist and speculator who farmed the royal mines in Wales, 1636–7.

Bussières, Jean de. Poet and historian. His *Flosculi historici delibati nunc delibatores redditi* ran to many editions, the first about 1649.

Butler, Charles. An advocate of spelling reform and author of several treatises on grammar and music. He taught at Basingstoke and was rector of Nately-Scures, Hampshire, 1593–1600. He died in 1647.

Calepino (Calepin), Ambrogio, 1435–1511. The Italian lexicographer and Augustinian monk. His polyglot dictionary was developed from his Latin–Italian dictionary of 1502.

Calvinius, Johannes. The lexicographer of Heidelberg whose *Lexicon Iuridicum Iuris Romani* was published in 1600.

Camden, William, 1551–1623. His *The Remains concerning Britain* was published in 1605.

Capgrave, John, 1393–1464. Theologian and historian. His principal works were *Nova Legenda Angliae, De illustribus Henricis* and *Vita Humfredi Ducis Glostriae.*

Carnarvon, Robert Dormer, first Earl of. The royalist commander during the Civil War who was killed at the battle of Newbury, 1643.

Caro, Annibale, born 1507. The Italian rhetorician and poet who published commentaries on Aristotle and the Latin authors in the later sixteenth century.

Carrington, Archibald Primrose, Lord, 1616–79. A follower of Montrose who was condemned for treason, 1646, but was released to join Charles II at the battle of Worcester. Though deprived of his estates during the Interregnum, he prospered at the Restoration, being rewarded with high legal office and membership of the privy council.

Case, John. Canon of Salisbury and Oxford scholar who practised medicine, published philosophical texts and commentaries on Aristotle. He died in 1601.

Castaneus (Henri Louis Chasteignier de la Rochepozay). His *Celebriorum distinctionum philosophicarum synopsis* appeared in 1657.

Castlemaine, Roger, Earl of, 1634–1705. A linguist and mathematician. He married Barbara Villiers in 1659.

Caus (Caulx), Salomon de, 1576–1626. Huguenot engineer and architect who lived in Germany and England. He is credited with the invention of the steam engine.

Chales, Claude François Milliot de. The mathematician and geographer, author of *L'art de Navigation*, 1677, and *Les Principes généraux de la Geographie*, 1677.

Charron, Pierre, 1541–1603. Friend of Montaigne. Though a catholic publicist, his chief work, *De la Sagesse*, 1601, challenges the validity of all forms of religion.

Cheke (Cheek), Sir John, 1514–57. Professor of Greek at Cambridge. He published several Greek texts and translations into the Latin.

Chester, Peyton, 1636–86. Brother of Sir Anthony Chester of Chicheley, Buckinghamshire.

Chiswell, Richard, the elder, 1639–1711. Publisher at the Rose and Crown, in St Paul's churchyard.

Clavius, Christopher, 1537–1612. Bavarian Jesuit astronomer and mathematician. He introduced the decimal point about 1593 and edited Euclid's *Elements*.

Cleland, James. Writer on courtly behaviour and the education of the nobility. *The institution of a young nobleman* was published in 1607 and *The instruction of a young nobleman* in 1612.

Cluverius (Philip Cluver), 1580–1622. The German antiquarian and geographer.

Cluverus, Dethlevus. Aubrey's friend and one of the early fellows of the Royal Society, elected November, 1678.

Coke, Sir Edward, 1552–1634. Speaker of the House of Commons, 1593, judge and legal writer.

Colbert, Jean Baptiste, 1619–83. Louis XIV's minister of finance.

Colerus, Johannes. A preacher at Parchim who wrote on farming, husbandry and domestic economics. His *Calendarum oeconomicum et perpetuum* was published in 1592.

Coley, Henry. Mathematician and astronomer. His *Clavis astrologiae; or, a key* was published in 1669.

Collins, John, 1625–83. Mathematics teacher in London and member of the Royal Society.

Collins, Samuel, 1576–1651. Provost of King's College, Cambridge, 1615, and Regius Professor, 1617–51.

Columella, Lucius Junius Moderatus. Roman writer on agriculture in the first century, A.D., the author of *De re rustica*.

Comenius, J. Amos, 1592–1670. The Moravian educationist who was invited to England in 1641 to undertake the reform of the educational system. His theories were embodied in his *Didactica Magna*, but in addition he wrote several important texts on language teaching, including *Ianua Linguarum*, 1631 and *Orbis Sensualium Pictus*, 1654.

Compton, Henry, Bishop of London, 1632–1713. Younger son of Spencer Compton, second Earl of Northampton.

Constantinus (Constantine VII), known as Porphyrogenitus, 905–959.

Cooper (Couper or Cowper), Thomas, 1517?–1594. He was master of Magdalen College School, Bishop of Lincoln and Winchester. His *Thesaurus Linguae Romanae*, published in 1565, was known as Cooper's *Dictionary*.

Corderius (Mathurin Cordier), 1479–1564. A French catholic teacher who was converted to protestantism and settled in Geneva. His *Colloquies*, widely used in English schools, were known as the *Cordery*.

Cotgrave, Randle. Scholar of St John's College, Cambridge, and secretary to William Cecil, second Earl of Exeter. He died in 1634.

Cowley, Abraham, 1618–67. The poet, whose *Propositions for the Advancement of Experimental Philosophy*, 1661, anticipated the foundation of the Royal Society.

Craddock, Samuel, 1621?–1706. Congregational divine and author of theological works who kept an academy at Geesings in Suffolk.

Craven, William, Earl of, 1606–97. Eldest son of Sir William Craven, Lord Mayor of London, 1610. He fought on the continent in the service of Maurice, Prince of Orange, 1623, and was with Prince Rupert at the battle of Limegea in 1637. He lost his estates to parliament during the Civil War but recovered his former position in 1660 and was created Viscount Craven of Uffington and Earl of Craven in 1664. He was one of the early members of the Royal Society.

Crooke, Andrew. King's printer and bookseller in Dublin, 1681–1731, the son of John Crooke, 1638–69. In the 1680s he was in partnership with his mother Mary; in 1685 he joined forces with Samuel Helsham as a printer.

Crumham (Cromleholme or Crumlam), Samuel. Schoolmaster of St Paul's School, 1657–72.

Dachetus (Dachety), Petrus. His *Almanack* was published in 1556.

Danvers, Sir John, 1588?–1655. Colonel in the parliamentary army, 1642, regicide and member of the council of state, 1649–53.

Davenant, Edward, 1596–1680. Mathematician, prebendary of Salisbury, kinsman of John Davenant. He taught algebra and in Wren's opinion was the outstanding mathematician of his generation. He was father-in-law to Aubrey's close friend, Anthony Ettrick.

Davys (Davies), John, 1625–93. Rector of Mallywd, Merioneth, 1604–8, and prebendary of Asaph. A philologist and translator of books of exploration of the Frenchman, Vigueford.

Dee, John, 1527–1608. Mathematician and astronomer of Trinity College, Cambridge, who lectured at Paris and Louvain. His geographical and hydrological works were sponsored by Queen Elizabeth. Latterly, his search for the philosopher's stone and his attempts to get in touch with angels brought imputations of his being a magician.

Despodius (Dasypodius), C. His edition of Euclid, *Euclidis Elementorum liber primus* was published in 1571.

Digby, Simon, 1648?–1720. A graduate of Trinity College, Dublin, 1664, he became bishop of Limerick in 1678 and of Elphin in 1691.

Digges, Leonard. Mathematician of University College, Oxford. He died about 1571.

Digges, Thomas. Son of Leonard Digges. He published some of his father's works and himself wrote on applied mathematics.

Diodati, Giovanni, 1576–1649. Swiss theologian who published Italian and French translations of the Bible.

Diophantus, of Alexandria. Mathematician, and reputedly the first algebraist. Various authorities place his career between A.D. 160 and 360.

Doderidge, Sir John, 1555–1628. M.P. for Horsham, Sussex, between 1603 and 1611, Solicitor General in 1604 and a justice of King's Bench in 1612. His principal legal work, *The English Lawyer*, was published in 1631.

Donne, John, 1573–1631. The poet. His *Devotions upon emergent occasions* was published in 1624.

Dorset, Charles Sackville, sixth Earl of, 1638–1706. Poet and leader, with Sir Charles Sedley, of the fashionable profligate circle of the post-Restoration period. He was a commander in the naval war against the Dutch in 1665 and attained high office under William III, acting on three occasions as regent during the King's absence.

Dousa, Janus (Jan van der Does), 1545–1604. The Dutch author of commentaries on Latin classical authors. He was one of the political leaders in the struggle against Philip II of Spain. His *Annals of Holland* was published in 1599.

Drexilius, Hieremias. French writer of the early seventeenth century. His *Angel-guardian's clock* was published in 1621, *Considerations upon eternity* in 1632 and *The school of patience*, 1640. The text Aubrey recommends, *Aurifodina artium et scientarum omnium*, came out in 1632.

Dryden, John, 1631–1700. The poet. His *Spanish Friar*, an attack on papists, was published in 1681.

Dugres (du Gres), Gabriel. A Huguenot refugee in the 1630s who taught French at both Oxford and Cambridge. He is best known for his *Regulae Pronunciandi*, 1652.

Duranti (Guillaume Durand), 1237?–96. French prelate and jurist.

Durie (Dury), John, 1596–1680. A protestant divine who travelled widely in his efforts to bring about the unification of the evangelical churches of Western Europe. He was a close associate of Hartlib and the author of several works on education including *The Reformed School*, 1650 and *Some Proposals towards the Advancement of Learning*, 1653.

Dydimus (Didymus). The blind ecclesiastical writer of Alexandria in the fourth century A.D.

Elyot, Sir Thomas, 1490?–1546. The diplomatist, ambassador and political theorist who was much influenced by the humanist doctrines of Erasmus. His *Boke called the Gouvenour* was published in 1531.

Ettmueller, Michael, 1644–83. A ubiquitous traveller and teacher with a high reputation in the seventeenth century as a pathologist and pharmaceutical chemist.

Ettrick, Anthony, 1622–1703. One of Aubrey's closest friends.

Farnaby, Thomas, 1575?–1647. Schoolmaster of Goldsmiths' Alley, London. He sailed with Drake and Hawkins, was a friend of G. J. Vossius and Ben Jonson and co-operated with Meric Casaubon in an edition of Terence.

Fell, John, Bishop of Oxford, 1625–86. Vice-Chancellor of Oxford, 1666–9 and Bishop of Oxford, 1675. He was the butt of Tom Brown's epigram 'I do not like you, Dr Fell.'

Feltmannus (Feltman), Gerhardus. Legal writer in the second half of the seventeenth century.

Finch, Sir John, 1584–1660. Speaker of the House of Commons and Lord Keeper.

Finckelthaus, Sigismund, 1580–1644. Professor of law and rector of the university of Leipzig.

Firmat (Fermat), Pierre de, 1601–65. French mathematician who explored probabilities and the properties of numbers. He is regarded as the inventor of differential calculus. His manuscripts were published in 1679 by his son under the title *Varia Opera Mathematica*.

Firmin (Fourmin), Thomas, 1632–97. The philanthropist whose practical schemes of self-help for the poor included a linen factory in Little Britain, established in 1676.

Fitzherbert, Sir Anthony, 1470–1538. Judge. His *La Graunde Abridgement*, an attempt to systematize the law, was published in 1514.

Flamsteed, John, 1646–1719. The first Astronomer Royal, a clergyman and a member of the Royal Society.

Fleetwood, Sir Miles, 1535?–94. Recorder of London, 1571, and M.P. for the City.

Florio, John. An early writer on the English language. *Florio, his first fruits; a perfect introduction to the Italian and English tongues* was published in 1578 and *A worlde of wordes; or, dictionarie in Italian and English* in 1598.

Flud, Thomas. The antiquarian friend of Aubrey and of Edward, Lord Herbert of Cherbury.

Foley, Richard, 1580–1657. The iron manufacturer of Stourbridge, originally of humble origins, whose considerable fortune was based on his discovery in Sweden of the secret 'splitting' process (not, as Aubrey has it, in Spain).

Foley, Samuel, 1655–95. Son of Samuel Foley of Clonmell, Co. Tipperary; educated at Trinity College, Dublin. He was a member of the Dublin Philosophical Society which modelled its scientific and experimental work on the Royal Society. Foley was one of the founder members. He became bishop of Down and Connor in 1694.

Fournier, P. Georg, 1595–1652. Son of Claude Fournier of Caen. He was a teacher at the Jesuit college at La Flèche and professor of law at Caen. His *Euclidis sex priores elementorum geometricorum libri demonstrati* was published in 1643. He wrote also on geography and fortifications.

Frigus (Freigus or Freig), John Thomas, 1543–83. Born at Fribourg, son of Nicolas Freig. His principal works were *De moribus veterum Gallorum*, 1574, *Vie latine de Ramus*, 1574, *Praelectiones in orationes*, 1580, *Quaestiones physicae*, 1579, and *Grammatica latina*, 1580.

Gale, Thomas. High master of St Paul's School, 1672–97. An active member of the Royal Society and at one time professor of Greek at Cambridge.

Galen. The Greek physician who emigrated to Rome from Asia Minor in the second century A.D.

Gardiner, William. Aubrey's schoolmaster at Blandford. He appears to have followed William Sutton there in 1632 and to have had the school for four years until his death in 1636. Possibly the William Gardiner who graduated from Hart Hall, Oxford in 1578.

Gellius, Aulus. The Latin writer of the second century A.D. His *Noctes Atticae* is a repository of information on ancient customs, language and philosophy.

Gerard, John, 1545–1612. The herbalist. His *Herball* appeared in 1597.

Goad, John. Fellow of St John's College, Oxford, in 1632 and former headmaster of Tonbridge School. He had Merchant Taylors' School from 1661 until 1681 when he was ousted for harbouring Roman Catholic tendencies.

Gotofredus (Gothofredus), Johann Philipp Abelin. The German historian whose *Theatrum Europaem*, 1633–8, was an illustrated history in serial form.

Grantham, Thomas. The rector of Waddington in Lincolnshire and London schoolmaster whose progressive views on education and attacks on the grammar schools and on corporal punishment brought him some notoriety. Around 1644 he set up a school in Bow Lane and another in Mugwell Street. He wrote, *inter al.*, *The Brain Breaker's Breaker, A Discourse . . . of the teaching in Free Schools and other Common Schools*, and *The Brain Breaker's Breaker newly broke out again*. He died in 1664.

Gravius (Gravius or Grave), Johann Georg, 1632–1703. The editor of several classical authors and historiographer to William III.

Greatrex, Ralph. The mathematical instrument maker and friend of Oughtred, Pepys and Evelyn. He died around 1712.

Greene, Robert, 1560?–92. Pamphleteer, poet and playwright.

Grotius, Hugo, 1583–1645. The Dutch jurist, dramatist and statesman whose *De Jure Belli et Pacis*, 1625, is regarded as the first real attempt at a systematic study of international law.

Grotius, William. The younger brother of Hugo Grotius. His principal work was *De principis juris naturalis enchiridion*, 1667, published posthumously. He died in 1662.

Guildford, Francis North, first Baron, 1637–85. Lord Chancellor, 1682. A patron of science and the arts in the post-Restoration period.

Gunning, Peter, Bishop of Ely, 1614–84. A staunch royalist who continued to hold episcopalian services throughout the Interregnum and became after the Restoration master of Clare and St John's colleges and Bishop of Chichester. He held Ely from 1675 to 1684.

Gunter, Edmund, 1581–1626. Mathematician and Gresham professor of astronomy, 1619–26.

Haak, Theodore, 1605–90. A Dutch immigrant who came to England in 1625. With Abraham Cowley, he is credited with proposals which led to the foundation of the Royal Society.

Hale, Sir Matthew, 1609–76. Counsel for Archbishop Laud at his impeachment and during the Commonwealth period sergeant-at-law and justice of common pleas. He figured prominently in the Convention parliament, 1660 and became Lord Chief Justice in 1671.

Halifax, George Savile, Marquis of, 1633–95. Son of Sir William Savile of Thornhill, Yorkshire. M.P. for Pontefract, statesman and author of the *Character of a Trimmer*, a political tract urging Charles II to thwart the claim to the throne of his brother James by advancing those of the Duke of Monmouth. He was instrumental in securing the succession of William and Mary after James fled in 1688.

Hall, John, 1627–56. Poet and political pamphleteer; an associate of Hartlib. He left Cambridge University in 1647 and, seeking preferment, composed his *An Humble Motion*, 1649, urging parliamentary reform of education. His energies were rewarded with a pension of £100 a year.

Halley, Edmund, 1656–1742. The Astronomer Royal, 1721.

Hampden, John, 1594–1643. The parliamentary leader who with Sir John

Eliot and John Pym led the opposition to Charles I's financial measures.

Harley, Sir Edward, 1624–1700. Distinguished parliamentary soldier and governor of Dunkirk. After the Restoration he opposed the legislation against nonconformists and published several theological works.

Harley, Thomas. An early fellow of the Royal Society, elected May 1667.

Harpsfield, Nicholas, 1519–75. Theologian and professor of Greek.

Harrington, James, 1611–77. Political theorist.

Harriot (Herriot), Thomas, 1560–1621. Astronomer and mathematical tutor to Sir Walter Raleigh, 1580. His principal work, *Artis analyticae praxis aequationes algebraicas resolvendas*, was edited in 1631 by Walter Warner.

Hartlib, Samuel. Of Polish origin, he came to England in 1628. He popularized the works of Comenius in England and had a hand in most of the educational ventures of the 1640s and 1650s. He died around 1670.

Helvicius, Christophorus, 1581–1617. The celebrated philologist. A child prodigy as a linguist; he studied at Marburg and produced in addition to *Christian Dialogues* several other works including *Grammatica Latina*, 1615, and a universal grammar.

Henley, Anthony, 1650?–1711. Son of Robert Henley of the Grange, Hampshire; a student of Christ Church and Middle Temple; a noted wit and patron of the arts who sat as Whig M.P. for Andover. He was a prominent member of the political Kit-Cat Club.

Henley, Sir Robert. Son of Sir Robert, master of the court of King's Bench. M.P. for Andover, 1679. He married Barbara, daughter of Sir Edward Hungerford, and lived at the Grange, near Alresford, Hampshire, where Aubrey was a frequent visitor.

Herbert, Arthur, Earl of Terrington, 1647–1715. He entered the navy in 1663 and fought against the Dutch, French and the Mediterranean corsairs.

Herbert, Edward, first Baron Herbert of Cherbury, 1583–1648.

Herbert, Sir Edward, 1591?–1657. Cousin of Edward Herbert. He was Solicitor-general in 1640 and Attorney-general in 1641.

Herigon (Herigone), Pierre. His *Cursus mathematicus nova* of 1634 was a compendium of works on Euclid, on arithmetic and trigonometry.

Hertford, Edward Seymour, Earl of, 1539–1621. He was the son of Edward Seymour, Duke of Somerset, 1506–52.

Hesse-Cassel, William VI of. The third Landgrave of the elder line of the house of Hesse, founded in 1567 by William the Wise.

Hill, Abraham, 1635–1721. Treasurer of the Royal Society, 1663–5 and 1679–1700.

Holder, William, 1616–98. Canon of St Paul's and tutor to Christopher Wren. His *Elements of Speech* was published in 1669.

Holland, Philemon, 1552–1637. Master of the grammar school at Coventry and translator of Livy, Pliny, Plutarch and Suetonius.

Hollar, Wenceslaus, 1607–77. Engraver and teacher of drawing to Prince Charles, afterwards Charles II.

Holles, Lord Denzil, 1599–1680. One of the five members impeached in 1642. He was ambassador at Paris from 1663 to 1666.

Holwell, John, 1649–1686? Astrologer and mathematician whose *A Sure Guide to the Practical Surveyor* was published in 1678.

Holyoke (Holyoake), Francis, 1567–1633. The lexicographer. His *Dictionarium Etymologicum Latinum* was published in 1633.

Hooke, Robert, 1635–1703. Son of a clergyman on the Isle of Wight. He was associated with Wilkins, Petty, Boyle, Wren and others at Oxford from whose number the Royal Society evolved. An outstanding mathematician and inventive genius whose creations ranged from sundials and iris diaphragms to compound microscopes.

Hoole, Charles, 1610–67. Master of the school at Rotherham until the outbreak of the Civil War. He became a private schoolmaster in London at Aldersgate and Lothbury. His teaching methods, acclaimed by his contemporaries, are set out in his *A New Discovery of the old Art of Teaching School*, 1660.

Hopton, Ralph, first Baron, 1598–1652. The royalist commander in the south and west during the Civil War.

Horneck, Anthony, 1641–97. A German immigrant vicar of All Saints, Oxford, 1671, and preacher at the Savoy, the nefarious sanctified London franchise and resort of criminals whom the law (before the Act of 1697) could not touch.

Hoskins (Hoskyns), Sir John, 1634–1705. Barrister of the Middle Temple and president of the Royal Society, 1682–3.

Howell, James, 1594–1666. The author and pamphleteer whose private excursions in Holland, France and Italy and diplomatic missions to Spain and Sardinia provided the basis of his *Instructions for Forreigne Travel*, 1642.

Hussey, Thomas. Friend of Evelyn, the diarist, who had an estate at Sutton in Shere, near Wotton.

Isaacson, Henry, 1581–1654. The theologian and chronologer. His *Saturni Ephemerides* was published in 1633.

Jenkins, Sir Leoline, 1623–85. M.P. for Hythe and Oxford University in the 1670s. He was an associate of Sheldon and a judge of the prerogative court at Canterbury, judge of the admiralty court and a secretary of state, 1680–4.

Jhesus Sirac, fl. 200 B.C. Supposed author of the Apocryphal book *Ecclesiasticus*.

Jonson, Ben, 1573?–1637. Poet and dramatist.

Jungius, Joachim, 1587–1657. German philosopher and botanist and opponent of scholasticism. His *Logica Hamburgensis* was published in 1638. His *Isagoge Phytoscopica* was a taxonomy which served later as a model for Linnaeus.

Kennett, White, Bishop of Peterborough, 1660–1728. A historian, philologist and topographer with interests similar to Aubrey's. Like Aubrey he was associated with Anthony Wood, before becoming vice-principal of St Edmund Hall in 1691, prebendary of Salisbury in 1701 and dean of Peterborough in 1708. He is remembered for his *Compleat History of England*.

Kepler, Johannes, 1571–1630. The German astronomer.

Kersey, John, 1616–90. An associate of John Collins, who published works on algebra. He was a teacher of mathematics in London.

Kettle, Ralph, 1563–1643. Third president of Trinity College, Oxford, 1579.

Kynaston, Sir Francis, 1587–1642. Poet and member of parliament. He formed his learned academy, the Museum Minervae, in 1635.

La Hier (Hire), Laurent de, 1606–56. The French painter who was patronized by Richelieu.

Lairesse, Gerard de, 1640–1711. Dutch painter and etcher who wrote *Art of Painting*, 1690.

Lambert, John, 1619–83. Parliamentary commander in the north of England during the Civil War and one of Cromwell's major generals. He was tried for treason in 1662, convicted and imprisoned in Guernsey till his death in 1683.

Lambin (Lambinus), Denis, 1516–72. The French philologist.

Lassalls (Lassels), Richard, 1603–68. Roman catholic divine and professor of classics at the English college at Douai. His account of travels in Italy was published in 1670.

Latimer, Robert. Master of the private school at Malmesbury where Thomas Hobbes studied before going to Magdalen Hall, Oxford.

Lawes, William. Composer. He wrote the music for James Shirley's masque, *Triumph of Peace*, 1634. A royalist, he was killed in the fighting at Chester in 1645.

Leech, Sir Edward. Father-in-law of Aubrey's friend, Sir James Long.

Leicester, Philip Sidney, third Earl of, 1619–98.

Lely, Sir Peter, 1618–80. Portrait painter.

Leovitius (Leowitz), Cyprianus von. The German astronomer of the second half of the sixteenth century. His *Astrological catechism*, translated by Robert Turner, was published in England in 1657.

Lessius, Leonard, 1554–1623. The Flemish Jesuit historian.

L'Estrange, Roger, 1616–1704. Journalist, pamphleteer and author.

Leybourn, William, 1626–1700? Mathematician and schoolmaster. He was the author of several books on astronomy, surveying and practical arithmetic.

Libarius, Andreas. Doctor of Medicine, born at Halle in Saxony, he became rector of the college at Courbourg in 1605. His experiments led him to an interest in the processes of aging and in the chemistry of metals. His principal works were *Histoire de Métaux* and *Epistolarum chymicarum libri tres*, 1595. He died in 1616.

Licetus, Fortunius (Fortunatus). A prolific writer on philosophy, religion and mathematics in the first half of the seventeenth century. He wrote occasionally under the pseudonym Couradus van Roel.

Lipsy (Lipse), Juste, 1547–1606. The philologist, born at Isque, near Brussels. He was a professor of history at Leyden, 1577, and wrote prolifically on history, moral philosophy and politics.

Littleton, Sir Edward, 1589–1645. Chief Justice, 1640, and Lord Keeper, 1641.

Lloyd, William, Bishop of Asaph, 1627–1717. Successively Bishop of Asaph, of Lichfield and Coventry and of Worcester, he was one of the seven bishops accused in 1688 of publishing a seditious libel against the king. A considerable scholar and writer of sermons and pamphlets, he was encouraged by Burnet to undertake his *History of the Reformation of the Church of England*.

Long, Sir James, 1617–92. Nephew of Sir Robert Long.

Long, Sir Robert. Chancellor of the Exchequer, 1660–7. He died in 1673.

Loss, Friedrich. Physician and medical writer. His *Conciliorum sive de morborum curationibus* was published in 1684; *Observationum medicinalium libri quatuor* in 1672.

Lovelace, John, third Baron, 1638?–93.

Lovell, Robert, 1630?–90. The botanist. His *Enchiridion Botanicum* was published in 1659.

Lowe, Sir Gabriel, 1575–1659. Son of Sir Thomas Lowe, Lord Mayor of London, 1604. He was admitted to Gray's Inn, 1594.

Lubinus, Elhardus (Eilhard), 1565–1621. The German associate of Hartlib and Comenius in the campaign for reformed language teaching. Hartlib's *The True and Readie Way to Learne the Latine Tongue* is largely by Lubinus.

Lulle, Raimond, 1235–1315. The Christian philosopher, celebrated for his method, *Ars Lulliana*, a scheme for the systematic solution of all problems and a device for the acquisition for further knowledge, which held sway in Europe till amended by the Jesuit teachers and by Descartes in the sixteenth century. In addition to his works on scholastic philosophy, he wrote on mathematics, grammar, theology, astronomy and medicine. He was canonized in 1419.

Lumley, Richard, first Earl of Scarborough, 1650?–1721. Grandson of Richard Lumley, first Viscount Lumley of Waterford. Although educated as a Roman Catholic he became a protestant in 1687, supported William of Orange after the revolution of 1688 and fought at the battle of the Boyne. He was created Viscount Lumley in 1689 and Earl of Scarborough in 1690.

Maffei, Giovanni Pietro. Jesuit historian. His *Historiarum Indicarum* ... *selectarum item ex India Epistolarum* was published in 1588.

Magnus, John. Archbishop of Uppsala around 1550. His *Historia* ... *de omnibus Gothorum Sueonumque Regibus* was published in 1554.

Makin, Bathsua. The sister of John Pell and tutoress to the daughter of Charles I. She is thought to have kept a school at Putney around 1649. Her treatise on female education was published in 1673.

Malapertius, Carolus. Jesuit writer and mathematician of Douay in the early seventeenth century. His principal work, *Arithmeticae practicae brevis institutio*, was published in 1633.

March, John, 1612–57. Legal writer in the Commonwealth period. His *Actions for Slander* was published in 1648.

Mariana, Juan de, 1536–1623. Spanish Jesuit historian.

Mariet, Thomas. High Sheriff of Warwickshire. He had known Aubrey at Trinity and later shared chambers with him in the Middle Temple. Like Aubrey, he was a member of the Rota, the political debating club founded by James Harrington.

Markham, Gervase, 1568–1637. Soldier, linguist and writer on agriculture. He is said to have introduced the first Arab horse into England.

Martindale, Adam, 1623–86. Educated in the St Helens area between 1630 and 1639, he was prevented from going to Oxford by the Civil War and served instead as a clerk in the parliamentary army. Afterwards he became a minister and one of the outstanding teachers of mathematics of his day.

Martino, John. See Siliceus.

Martinus, Martinius, 1614–61. A Jesuit geographer and oriental historian who went on two missionary expeditions to China. The geographical dictionary was probably the *Atlas sinensis*, 1655.

Mayerne, Sir Theodore Turquet de, 1573–1655. French physician to James I and Charles I.

Maynard, Sir John, 1602–90. Judge and barrister of the Middle Temple and Lord Commissioner of the Great Seal, 1689.

Mercator, Nicholas (Nicholas Kauffman), 1640–87. The German inventor and clockmaker.

Mercurialis, Hieronymus. A copious writer on medicine and editor of the works of Hippocrates. His *De arte gymnastica* was published in 1573.

Merry, Thomas, presumably Thomas Merriot, 1589–1662. Fellow of New College and vicar of Swalecliffe, around 1664, where he taught school. He was the author of several Latin works.

Meursius, Johannes, 1579–1639. Dutch classical philologist and antiquary.

Molineaux, William, 1656–98. A graduate of Trinity College Dublin, lawyer, mathematician and a member of the Royal Society, 1685. He published works on philosophy and optics.

Monteage, Stephen, 1623–87. A merchant and publisher of works on accounting. He was agent to Christopher Hatton, first Viscount Hatton, 1623–1706, the governor of Guernsey after the Restoration.

Morden, Robert. Geographer, publisher and map maker. He died about 1705.

More, Henry, 1614–87. One of the Cambridge Platonists.

More (Moore), Sir Jonas, 1617–79. Surveyor and mathematician, knighted in 1663 and appointed Surveyor-general of Ordnance. He published several mathematical treatises including *Arithmetick*, 1650 and a *New System of the Mathematics*, published after his death.

Moreland, Sir Samuel, 1625–95. Inventor, mathematician and diplomatist who served both parliament and Charles II. He produced calculating machines, a speaking-trumpet and experimented with steam as a source of power.

Morgan, Sir Anthony, 1621–68. Graduate of Magdalen, Oxford, 1641, and soldier, first in the royalist army and then in parliament's.

Moxon, Joseph, 1627–1700. Mathematician and hydrographer. His *Mechanick Exercises* was published in 1678.

Mulcaster, Richard, 1530?–1611. The first headmaster of Merchant Taylors' School, London, 1561–68, and at the turn of the century high master of St Paul's School. His *Elementarie*, a plea for English teaching, was published in 1582, a year after his *Positions*, which set out the case for mathematics teaching.

Mydorgius (Claude Mydorge). The French mathematician whose two books on conical sections were translated by William Oughtred in 1660. His *Les Recréations Mathématiques* was published in 1661.

Needlar, John. Born at Horley, Surrey, around 1601. He matriculated at Christ's College, Cambridge, 1617, and was admitted to Gray's Inn, 1634.

Neile, Sir Paul, 1628–86. Son of Richard Neile, Archbishop of York, 1631–40, and father of the mathematician, William, 1637–70.

Newport, Mountjoy Blount, first Earl of, 1597–1666. Natural son of Charles Blount, Earl of Devonshire, by Penelope, Lady Rich. A royalist commander during the Civil War.

Newton, John, 1622–78. A graduate of Edmund Hall, Oxford, 1642, and King's chaplain, 1661, who wrote on mathematics, astronomy and logic.

Norden, John, 1548–1625? Topographer and engineer, who also published devotional works.

Norwood, Richard, 1590?–1675. A teacher of mathematics in London and surveyor of islands controlled by the Bermuda Company, 1616. He is credited with the exact calculation of a degree of the meridian and in 1635 completed his measurement of the distance between York and London.

Ogilby, John, 1600–76. He was employed by Strafford in Ireland as a dancing master and as tutor to the Earl's children. After losing everything in the Civil War he eked out a living as usher in the school kept by James Shirley, the dramatist, in Whitefriars. He managed a theatre nearby and played some part in organizing the celebrations for the return of Charles II. Latterly, he set up as a bookseller and printer in Whitefriars.

Origen, A.D. 185?–254? Christian writer and teacher at Alexandria.

Osborne, Francis, 1593–1659. Master of the horse to William, third Earl of Pembroke and friend of Hobbes. In addition to his *Advice* he wrote memoirs of the reigns of Elizabeth and James I.

Oughtred, William, 1575–1660. A prolific writer on mathematics. He published his *Clavis Mathematicae* in 1631 and *Circles of Proportion* the following year. He is credited with the invention of trigonometrical abbreviations and with the signs for multiplication and proportion. His father, Benjamin, taught at Eton.

Overbury, Sir Thomas, 1581–1613. Poet and friend of Ben Jonson. The victim of court intrigue, implicated in Carr's Plot, 1613.

Owen, John, 1616–83. Theologian and Vice-Chancellor of Oxford, 1652–8.

Oxford, Aubrey de Vere, twentieth Earl of, 1626–1703. Son of Robert, nineteenth Earl, he was brought up in Friesland and served as a commander in Dutch service until 1648. A sequestered royalist, he had his estates restored in 1660 and became Lord Lieutenant of Essex. He opposed James II and fought in Ireland for William of Orange.

Pacii, Julius (Jules Pace), 1550–1635. The celebrated linguist and lawyer, born near Venice; he became a professor of civil law at Montpellier. In addition to his legal works, he wrote commentaries on Aristotle and on the *Ars Lulliana*.

Paget, Edward. Fellow of Trinity College, Cambridge, who was elected to the Royal Society in 1682. In the same year he was appointed to Christchurch Hospital School where his neglect almost brought a deadlock to the work of the foundation. He left the school in 1695.

Parkinson, John, 1567–1650. Apothecary and herbalist to James I.

Partridge, Sir Edward. Born 1601, son of Edward Partridge of Greenway Court in Kent. He was a student at Hart Hall and of Middle Temple. He became M.P. for Sandwich in 1640.

Paschal, Andrew, 1630–96. Rector of Chedsey, Somerset, around 1663. He corresponded regularly with Aubrey. Whilst at Cambridge he had occupied the rooms Erasmus had used at Queens' College.

Paullus, Simon. Professor at Rostock. His *Quadripartitium de simplicium medicamentorum facultatibus* was published in 1639.

Peacham, Henry, 1576?–1643? Schoolmaster at Wymondham; an engraver, author and mathematician who from 1613 was tutor to the sons of Thomas Howard, second Earl of Arundel.

Pelisson-Fontainer, Paul, 1624–93. Born at Béziers; studied law at Toulouse and became a member of the Académie française. In 1645 he published a Latin paraphrase of the *Institutes* of Justinian.

Pell, John, 1611–85. The mathematician associated with Hartlib in his attempt to set up an academy at Chichester. He taught in Sussex before becoming a professor of mathematics at Amsterdam and Breda. His *An Idea of Mathematics written by Mr John Pell to Samuel Hartlib* appeared in 1638.

Pembroke, Thomas Herbert, eighth Earl of, 1656–1733. Third son of Philip Herbert, fifth Earl, he succeeded his brothers to the title. He was Lord-Lieutenant of Wiltshire till 1687 and Lord Privy Seal, 1692.

Penn, William, 1644–1718. The quaker and founder of Pennsylvania.

Penton, Stephen, 1639–1706. Principal of St Edmund Hall, Oxford, 1676–1684. From 1693 until his death he was rector of Wath-by-Ripon.

Petty, Sir William, 1622–87. Political economist and demographer. He was professor of anatomy at Oxford, 1651, and one of the original members of the Royal Society.

Peyton, Robert. Younger brother of Sir John Peyton of Isleham, Cambridge, and vicar of Broad Chalke.

Philip IV of Spain, 1605–65. The eldest son of Philip III. The administration of the kingdom was left to his chief minister, Olivares (Gaspar de Guzman).

Philip (Philips), Henry. The author of *The Purchasers Pattern*, published in 1654.

Philipps, Fabian, 1601–90. Royalist sympathizer and author, who, at the Restoration, became Remembrancer of the Court of the Marches.

Phillips, Edward, 1630–96. The son of Milton's sister, Ann, whom Milton educated. In 1663 he became tutor to the son of John Evelyn, the diarist, and in 1665 to Philip Herbert, afterwards seventh Earl of Pembroke.

Pibrac (Gui Du Faur, Seigneur de Pibrac), 1529–84. Magistrate and poet, ambassador of Charles IX to the Council of Trent and Chancellor of Marguérite de Valois. His *Cinquante Quatrains* was published in 1574.

Pitfield, Alexander, 1658–1728. A barrister of Lincoln's Inn, member of the Royal Society, 1684 and M.P. for Bridport, 1698–1708.

Plattes (Platt), Sir Hugh, 1552–1608. Inventor and agriculturalist whose discoveries, set out in *The Jewel House of Art and Nature*, anticipated many of the improvements of the eighteenth century.

Plott, Robert, 1640–96. Secretary to the Royal Society, 1682, and first keeper of the Ashmolean Museum.

Plowden, Edmund, 1518–85. Jesuit, barrister of the Middle Temple.

Polyxfen (Pollexfen), Sir Henry, 1632–91. A successful barrister in the 1660s and Lord Chief Justice of Common Pleas, 1689.

Pope, Sir Thomas, 1507?–59. Founder of Trinity College, Oxford.

Popham, Alexander, 1605–69. Second son of Francis Popham, of Littlecote,

Wiltshire; a student of Balliol College and Middle Temple and M.P. between 1640 and 1660 for Bath, Wiltshire and Minehead.

Porta, Giovanni Baptista della. Neapolitan inventor and experimenter in optics. His review of natural phenomena, *Natural Magic*, was published in 1658; his *Villa*—an account of crop and farming experiments—in 1592.

Portman, Sir William, 1641?–90. The owner of large estates in the south and west of England. With Lord Lumley, he captured Monmouth in 1685 and joined William of Orange in 1688.

Potter, Hannibal, 1592–1664. President of Trinity College, Oxford, 1643–7, and again following 1660.

Povey, Thomas, fl. 1633–85. M.P. for Liskeard, Cornwall, in 1647; a friend of Evelyn and Pepys and the holder of a number of minor court offices under Charles II.

Powell, Griffith, 1561–1620. Principal of Jesus College, Oxford, 1613–20, and author of commentaries on Aristotle and the sophists.

Prideaux, John, Bishop of Worcester, 1578–1650. Vice-Chancellor of Oxford, 1619–21.

Prudentius, Marcus Aurelius Clemens. The Latin Christian writer, born in northern Spain in A.D. 348.

Prynne, William, 1600–69. Puritan pamphleteer and keeper of the records of the Tower of London.

Pufendorf, Baron Samuel von, 1632–94. The German jurist and historian who wrote under the pseudonym Severinus. His principal works were *De Jure Naturae et Gentium*, 1672, and *De Statu Imperii Germanici*, 1667.

Quintilian, Marcus Fabius Quintilianus. The Spanish rhetorician who taught in Rome around A.D. 70. His principal work, *Institutio Oratoria*, describes not only the curricula, but also the best teaching methods of Roman schools.

Ramus, Petrus (Pierre la Ramée), 1515–72. The French Catholic humanist and mathematician whose writings attacking Aristotle evoked much hostility in the mid-seventeenth century. He died, a protestant, in the massacre of St Bartholomew's Day.

Randall (Randolph), Thomas, 1605–35. Poet, dramatist and friend of Ben Jonson.

Ranelagh, Catherine Boyle, Viscountess, died 1691. One of the fifteen children of Richard Boyle, first Earl of Cork, 1566–1634. One of the most talented women of her age and advocate of educational reform.

Ray, John, 1627–1705. The naturalist. His *Collection of English Proverbs* was published in 1670.

Recorde, Robert, 1510–58. The first influential writer in English on mathematics.

Richardson, Alexander. A graduate of Queens' College, Cambridge, in 1584. He lived in Surrey. The first edition of *The Logician's Schoolmaster* was published in 1629.

Ridgeley, Luke, 1615–97. Son of Thomas Ridgeley, M.D., of Newark in Nottinghamshire. He was a graduate of St John's College, Cambridge, and M.R.C.P., 1617. He practised medicine in Bloomsbury.

Rochester, John Wilmot, second Earl of, 1648–80. The satirist and libertine.

Rolle, Henry, 1589–1656. Judge of King's Bench, 1645, Lord Chief Justice and member of the council of state during the Interregnum. Father of Sir Francis Rolle.

Rous, Francis, 1579–1659. Lawyer and M.P. for Truro in the Short and Long Parliaments; Provost of Eton, 1644, and Speaker of the House of Commons.

Salisbury, Earls of. William, died 1226, the first Earl of the Longespée family is unlikely to have been the subject of Aubrey's anecdote. More probably it was Robert, the first Earl of the Cecil family, 1563?–1612. (See Burghley.)

Sanderson, Robert, 1587–1663. Bishop of Lincoln.

Sandys, George, 1578–1644. Poet, traveller and courtier to Charles I. His work was much admired by Aubrey. The *Metamorphoses* was published in 1626, his *Paraphrase upon the Psalms* in 1636.

Savile, Henry, 1549–1622 Oxford mathematician and founder of the Savile professorships.

Scapula, Joannes. Born in the sixteenth century, he was employed in the printing house of Henri Estienne, and like Estienne was a Greek lexicographer. His lexicon is largely a plagiarized version of Estienne's thesaurus, published seven years earlier.

Scarborough, Sir Charles, 1616–94. Physician to Charles II, James II and Queen Mary and one of the original fellows of the Royal Society.

Schickard, William, 1592–1635. The German orientalist. He held a chair of Hebrew languages at Tübingen university in 1619.

Schottus, Gaspar. Jesuit writer on mechanics. His *Mechanica hydraulico pneumatica* was published in 1657.

Scottenius (Schottennius), Hermanus. The Bohemian Latin writer and educationist. His *Aureus libellus colloquioru* was published in 1535; the *Instructio prima puerorum* in 1527.

Scroderus (Schroeder), Johannus. Doctor of medicine at Frankfurt on Main. His *Pharmacopoeia* was published in 1684.

Selden, John, 1584–1654. The jurist.

Seller, John. Publisher of maps and hydrographer to Charles II. He was author of *The Art of Navigation*, *The English Pilot*, and *The Sea Atlas*, 1671.

Senhault (Senault), Jean François. The author of a number of devotional works including *The use of the passions*, 1649, *The Christian Man*, 1650, and *The natural history of the passions*, 1674.

Servius, Maurus Honoratus. The Latin writer of the late fourth and early fifth centuries, author of a commentary on Vergil.

Shaen, Sir James. One of the original fellows of the Royal Society, elected May 1663.

Shaftesbury, Anthony Ashley Cooper, first Earl of. (See Ashley.)

Sharrock (Shurrock), Robert. Writer on civil law. His *De officiis secundum naturae jus* was published in 1660; *De finibus virtutis Christianae* in 1673.

Sherwin, William. Son of William Sherwin, minister of Wallington. He was an engraver who, like Prince Rupert, was one of the first to work in mezzotint.

Siliceus, Johannes. Tutor to Philip II of Spain. He died in 1557. He wrote also under the names Martinus, Martino and Martinez.

Sleidan, Johannes, 1506–56. The German historian and diplomatic envoy of Francis I of France.

Smith (Smythe), Sir Robert. A contemporary and friend of John Evelyn at Balliol College, Oxford. He married Dorothy Spencer (see Sunderland, Dorothy Spencer) in 1652 after nine years of widowhood and lived with her at Sutton-at-Hone and at Boundes, near Penshurst in Kent.

Smith, Sir Thomas, 1513–77. Vice-Chancellor and professor of civil law at Cambridge University. He worked at Cambridge for the reform of Greek pronunciation.

Smythwick, Francis. One of the early fellows of the Royal Society, elected in April 1667, whose special interest was in the grinding of optical lenses.

Speed, John, 1552?–1629. Historian and cartographer.

Spelman, Sir Henry, 1564?–1641. A historian and antiquarian with interests similar to Aubrey's. He studied at Trinity College, Cambridge, and Lincoln's Inn. His works deal principally with ecclesiastical history and philology. In 1635 he established a readership in Anglo-Saxon at Cambridge.

Spencer, Sir John. Levant merchant and Lord Mayor of London. He died in 1610.

Spenser, Edmund, 1552?–1599. The poet.

Spiedell, Euclid. Possibly the brother of John Spiedell, the teacher of mathematics in London and author of *Geometrical Extractions*. His *Logarithmotechnia; or, the making of numbers* was published in 1688.

Sprat, Thomas, 1635–1713. Bishop of Rochester, 1684 and historian of the Royal Society.

Stephanus (Charles Estienne). His *Maison Rustique; or, the country farm*, with Jean Liebault, was published in 1600.

Stephens, Robert, 1665–1732. The historiographer and barrister of the Middle Temple.

Stevins (Stevinus), Symon, 1548–1620. Dutch mathematician and military engineer.

Stoeffler, Johann, 1452–1531. Mathematical professor at Tübingen.

Street, Thomas. A writer on the calendar and the planetary system. His *Astronomica Carolina* was published in 1661.

Strode, Thomas, d. 1688. Mathematician and horologist; his principal works were *A Short treatise of the combinations, elections, permutations and composition of quantities*, 1678, and *A new and easie method of the art of dyalling*, 1687.

Suarez, Francisco, 1548–1617. The Spanish Jesuit historian and philosopher.

Sunderland, Dorothy (Dorothea) Spencer, Countess of, 1617–84. She married Robert Smith in 1652. Her first husband, the Earl, died in 1643 of wounds received at the battle of Newbury. For some years before her first marriage she had been paid literary court by the poet, Edmund Waller.

Sympson, Nathanial, 1599–1642, author of the *Arithmetical Compendium*, 1622.

Tabernaemontanus (Johann Teodor), 1515–90. The German physician and botanist.

Thanet, Nicholas Tufton, Earl of. Aubrey's patron of Bobbing Place, Bobbing, in Kent where Aubrey was a constant visitor in the 1670s.

Tidmarsh, Samuel. Bookseller at the King's Head in Sweeting's Alley End, Cornhill, near the Royal Exchange, 1679–89; chiefly a publisher of works of divinity.

Tillotson, John, Archbishop of Canterbury, 1630–94. One of the finest preachers of his day as Dean of St Paul's, 1689, and Archbishop, 1691. A prolific writer, whose works include three lengthy sermons on the education of children.

Tomb (Tombes), John, 1603–76. The baptist divine, a popular preacher and the author of a number of religious tracts.

Tonge, Israel (Ezerel), 1621–80. The London schoolmaster and dupe of Titus Oates.

Tremouille, Henri-Charles, Duc de La, 1620–72. He was the son of Henri, Duc de La Tremouille: he became a soldier in the army of his Dutch uncle, Frederick Louis and married Amélie, daughter of the Landgrave of Hesse-Cassel. He distinguished himself fighting in the Fronde.

Triplett, Thomas, 1603–93. Schoolmaster at Dublin, 1642, and at Hayes after the Restoration. A prebendary of Westminster.

Tryon, Thomas, 1634–1703. One of the most colourful figures of the seventeenth century, a shepherd and hatter's apprentice who travelled in the West Indies and wrote on dietetics and mystical philosophy.

Tully. The Anglicized form of Tullius, commonly used in the seventeenth century to refer to Marcus Tullius Cicero, 106–43 B.C.

Tully, Servius Tullius, 578–34 B.C. The Etruscan sixth king of Rome.

Twysden, John, 1607–88. Physician, His chief work, *Medicina veterum vindicata*, was published in 1666.

Ulpianus, Domitius (Ulpian), 170?–228. The Roman jurist and author of legal treatises and commentaries.

Ussher, James, Archbishop of Armagh, 1581–1656.

Valla, Laurentius, 1406–57. The Roman teacher of the classics at Pavia and Milan who translated Xenophon, Herodotus and Thucydides.

Van Dyck, Sir Anthony, 1599–1641. Painter and etcher.

Van Helmont, John Baptist, 1577–1644. A physician with advanced views on nutrition and digestion; as a chemist, the first to distinguish gases distinct from air, and indeed the father of the word *gas*. He claimed to have an attendant genius which appeared to him in a crystal. He is accorded by some writers a greater place in the history of chemistry than his predecessor, Paracelsus.

Varen (Vareny), Bernhard, 1622–50? The German geographer and author of an account of Japan. His chief work was *Geographia Generalis*, 1650.

Varro, Marcus Terentius, 116–27 B.C. Roman writer on geography, politics, law, customs and agriculture.

Vaughan, John, third Earl of Carberry, 1640–1713. Styled, by courtesy, Lord Vaughan, from 1667.

Veal (Veel), Edward, 1632?–1708. A graduate of Christ Church, Oxford, 1654, and subsequently a minister in Ireland. He was minister of a church at Wapping, 1668, and taught in Stepney.

Vieta, Franciscus (François Viete), 1540–1603. Mathematician and privy-councillor to Henry IV.

Vigerus, Franciscus (François Viger). Born at Rouen; a classical scholar and translator of Eusebius. His *De idiotismis praecipuis linguae graecae* was published in 1632.

Vinnius (Petrus de Vinea or Pietro della Vigna), 1190–1249. The Italian jurist and minister of Emperor Frederick II.

Vives, Ludovicius, 1492–1540. The Spanish humanist and classical scholar.

Vlack (Vlacq), Adrian, 1600?–67. Dutch mathematician and publisher of logarithmic tables.

Vossius, Isaac, 1618–89. Son of Gerard Vossius, a prolific writer and editor of the classics. A canon of Windsor, 1673–89.

Vossius, John Gerard, 1577–1649. Professor of history at Leyden and Amsterdam. Canon of Canterbury, 1629.

Walker, Obadiah, 1616–99. Romanist, ejected from his fellowship at University College, Oxford, during the Interregnum; reinstated as master there in 1676, but again ejected in 1688. He lived in exile, writing on education and theology.

Walker, William, 1623–82. The author of one of the standard Latin texts, *The Treatise of English Particles*, 1673.

Waller, Edmund, 1606–87. Poet and member of parliament. His *Sacharissa*, 1635, was a literary courtship of Dorothy Spencer, Countess of Sunderland.

Waller, Richard. Fellow of the Royal Society, elected April 1681, and one of the possible sponsors of Aubrey's school.

Wallis, John, 1616–1703. Savilian professor of geometry at Oxford, 1649–1703.

Ward, John. Mathematician and private schoolmaster in London, an acquaintance of Aubrey who relied heavily on his experience as a successful teacher.

Ward, Seth, Bishop of Salisbury, 1617–89. Mathematician and member of the Royal Society.

Wase, Christopher, 1627–90. Ejected during the Interregnum but restored from exile through the good offices of Evelyn. From 1662 to 1668 he was master of Tonbridge School. Later, at Oxford, he collected information on the state of English education by means of a national questionnaire.

Webbe, Joseph. Physician and grammarian who taught in the Old Bailey, London, 1623. He was an advocate of teaching in the vernacular, and published a translation of Cicero's *Familiar Epistles*, 1620.

Weclock (Wheelocke), Abraham, 1593–1653. The linguist. He published a translation of *Chronologia Saxonica* and began an Anglo-Saxon dictionary.

Wertzung (Christoph Wirsung), 1500?–71. German doctor, born in Augsburg. He wrote *Arznen Buch*, 1568, and *Praxis Medicinae*, translated by J. Mosan, 1598.

Westphaling, Herbert, 1532?–1602. Bishop of Hereford, 1586, and Vice-Chancellor of Oxford, 1576–77.

Weymouth, Thomas Thynne, first Viscount, 1640–1714.

Wheare, Degore(y). First Camden reader in history at Oxford. His lectures, *De ratione methodo Legendi historias*, were published in 1623.

White, Thomas (Albio), 1593–1676. Roman catholic writer and theologian who wrote under various pseudonyms, Albius, Anglus and Blacloe. He was the brother of the mathematician, Richard White, whom Hobbes admired. His *Institutiones Sacrae* was published in 1652, *Obedience and Government* in 1655.

Whitlock (Whitelock), Bulstrode. His *Memorials of the English affairs* was published in 1659. Among his other works were memoirs and collections of speeches.

Wilkins, John, 1614–72. Bishop of Chester and one of the group which formed the Royal Society.

William of Malmesbury, *c.* 1090–1143. The librarian of Malmesbury Abbey where he was educated. His principal historical work, *Gesta Regum Anglorum*, was completed in 1125.

Williamson, Sir Joseph, 1633–1701. Lawyer and keeper of Charles II's library at Whitehall.

Windham (Wyndham), Sir Wadham, 1610–68. Judge of King's Bench, 1660–8.

Wing, Vincent, 1619–68. Astronomer and land surveyor. He published his *Astronomia Britannica* in 1652.

Wingate, Edmund, 1596–1656. Mathematician and tutor to Princess Henrietta Maria in Paris, around 1624. His principal mathematical work was *L'usage de la règle de proportion en arithmetique*, 1624, but he also wrote *An exact abridgement of all the Statutes in force and use from the beginning of Magna Carta.*

Withers, George, 1588–1667. Poet and pamphleteer.

Wood, Anthony, 1632–95. The diarist, antiquarian and historian who was associated with Aubrey while working on the *Athenae Oxoniensis*, a biographical dictionary of Oxford writers and bishops. Though Aubrey regretted his death, the two were frequently at loggerheads while Wood lived. From 1693 until shortly before his death he was expelled from Oxford for libelling Edward Hyde, first Earl of Clarendon.

Wood (Woods), Robert, 1622?–85. Mathematician and physician. Accountant-general of Ireland and a member of the Royal Society. He published *A New Al-moon-ac for Ever* in 1680.

Woodward, Hezekiah, 1590–1675. Nonconformist schoolmaster at Aldermanbury, around 1619, and vicar of Bray in 1649. His works include *A Child's Patrimony*, 1640, and *A Gate to the Sciences*, 1641.

Worcester, Edward Somerset, sixth Earl and second Marquis, 1601–67. A royalist who recovered most of his dispossessed estates at the Restoration and devoted much of his time to mechanical experiments. He published *Century of Inventions* in 1655.

Wotton, Sir Henry, 1568–1639. Diplomatist and poet. He travelled widely in the service of the Earl of Essex after 1595 and was ambassador to Venice under James I. Between 1624 and 1639 he was Provost of Eton.

Wotton, William, 1666–1727. Prebendary of Salisbury, 1705–26, and author of several theological works. His *Reflections upon Ancient and Modern Learning* was published in 1694. His education was described in Henry Wotton's *Essay on the Education of Children*, 1672.

Wright, Edward, 1558–1605. Hydrographer and mathematician.

Wyld (Wild), Edmund, 1616–96. Aubrey's close friend and patron who survived the vicissitudes of a manslaughter charge, plagues and law-suits and lived until almost the turn of the century.

Yarrington, Andrew. His principal work, *England's improvements*, was published in 1674. He also wrote *A coffee-house dialogue*, 1679, a tract against presbyterians, *A new map of the Town of Dunkirk*, 1681.

Zeigleri, Caspar, 1621–90. Born at Leipzig, he studied at Wittenberg and Leipzig universities. Following 1654 he held various chairs of law at Wittenberg.

Zouch, Richard, 1590–1661. Professor of civil law at Oxford, 1620–61.

Index